Aristotle's *Poetics*
for Screenwriters

Aristotle's *Poetics* for Screenwriters

Storytelling Secrets from the Greatest Mind in Western Civilization

Michael Tierno

hachette
BOOKS

NEW YORK   BOSTON

Hachette Books
Hachette Book Group
1290 Avenue of the Americas
New York, NY 10104
www.HachetteBookGroup.com

Printed in the United States of America

LSC-C

Originally published in trade by Hyperion.
First Hachette Books trade edition published in 2015.

20 19

Hachette Books is a division of Hachette Book Group, Inc.
The Hachette Books name and logo are trademarks of Hachette
Book Group, Inc.

The publisher is not responsible for websites (or their content)
that are not owned by the publisher.

Bibliographic Note:

The translation of Aristotle's *Poetics* is taken from *Aristotle's
Art of Poetry: A Greek View of Poetry and Drama,* translated
by Ingram Bywater, with an introduction and explanation by
W. Hamilton Fyfe (1940). It has been reprinted by permis-
sion of Oxford University Press.

Designed by Lynn Amft

ISBN: 978-0-7868-8740-8

For Judy, the love of my life

Aristotle's *Poetics* has become to Hollywood screenwriters what Sun-tzu's *The Art of War* is to Mike Ovitz. So what if it's more than 2,000 years old? 'It's 42 pages of simple, irrefutable truths and the best book on screenwriting,' says writer-director Gary Ross (*Pleasantville*), who used *Poetics* as a text in classes he taught at UCLA and at the University of Southern California.

—*Entertainment Weekly*, cover story, June 29, 1999

Acknowledgments

First, heartfelt thanks to my wife Judy, my favorite person on earth. Her contributions to my life and this work are incalculable.

I am grateful to Hyperion. Because of the editors' swift response to this project and support throughout all phases of it, I can't complain one iota anymore that the powers that be don't think Aristotle is cool. I am grateful to Alison Lowenstein for signing the book and, when she left, handing it to Cassie Mayer, who has turned out to be a true collaborator. Her comments, queries, line edits, rearranging of chapters, and even ideas about movies to use were so on the money and inspiring that they pushed me deeper into the *Poetics* than I ever thought possible. They're the reason the book is more than I dreamed it could be.

Likewise, I am much indebted to my agent, Susan Crawford, who for no reason other than that this project sounded good, jumped on board and made it happen. Her disciplined guidance with the proposal is the principal reason you're reading this book.

I am grateful to the College of Staten Island, and especially to the City University of New York City Film School, which introduced me to cinema studies. This great institution successfully marries academic film studies with hands-on filmmaking, covering everything from semiotics to classical Hollywood and experimental cinema theory. My experience at the CUNY film school was greatly enhanced by outstanding professors: Mirella Affron, Sarah Kozloff, Richard Pena, Elaine Mancini, Phill Niblock, and Lenny Quart. They gave everything they had to ensure that my fellow students and I received a rich, solid filmmaking and cinema theory education.

Two other professors I've had the fortune of learning from are Martha Nussbaum and Stephen Halliwell. I was delighted they took time to answer my e-mails, as they are two of the top Aristotle scholars of all time. I recommend your reading as much of their writings as possible. I'd also like to acknowledge Films For The Humanities for giving me a video copy of *Oedipus Rex* to use as my basis for understanding Aristotle's favorite play.

My thanks, too, for the Writer's Room, because it gave me a place to go to help stave off the feeling of isolation that comes with writing. And to my dear friends Judith Nelson, Catharine Carlin, Toni L. Kamins, Harold Itzkowitz, and Eric Justice, all of whom gave me a lot of support through various phases of this project.

The movie business is tough to break into. Miramax Films gave me an opportunity to be a story analyst, and I'm especially grateful to Heidi Herman for taking the time to teach me the ropes and to Hannah Minghella and Tony Mosher for piling on all kinds of work as well as giving me a break to write this book. I am indebted to Jack Lechner and Sam Maser, who have given me a great deal of guidance and encouragement, and to my lawyer and friend, Robert L. Seigel, who has supported my filmmaking efforts, offering legal advice about and insight into the independent-film business. I am very grateful for the awe-inspiring New York Public Library, my favorite place on earth. Because of it, I feel like a billionaire.

Finally, my gratitude to my family for their love. And at the risk of sounding hokey, I am indebted to Aristotle because of the beautiful truth he left behind for anyone to stumble upon in his writings.

Contents

Contents

Preface

If, scarily enough, your screenplay happens to get read by a Hollywood studio, the story analyst will sum it up using a "coverage" form that looks something like this:

Log Line:
Brief:
Plot Summary:
Comments:
Idea:
Story:
Character:
Dialog:
Production Values:

Absolutely everything submitted to a Hollywood studio is boiled down to its bare merits and discussed using these nine topics of analysis. The form allows a story analyst to write a quick summary of the screenplay before zipping said summary off to an overworked story editor, who sends it to an equally time-taxed studio executive. Based on this coverage sheet, the executive decides whether or not to look at your script. What the items on the sheet represent are the no-brainer essentials of a screenplay—its idea, its story, and so forth. But you'd be surprised to find out that the criteria Hollywood executives use to evaluate screenplays are *exactly* those the legendary philosopher Aristotle thought were the nuts and bolts of ancient drama more than 2,000 years ago!

Aristotle carefully examined the fundamentals of dramatic story structure in the *Poetics*, which is still considered to be "the bible of screenwriting" by many Hollywood professionals today. Sharing this view, I use the *Poetics* as a guide to write scripts and make films, and have used its truths to analyze and write screenplay coverage notes as a story analyst for Miramax Films. Since the *Poetics* has helped me immensely in both endeavors, I feel obliged to share its insights with anyone interested in writing better screenplays.

Don't worry, this book is not an academic study. It's an introduction to the *Poetics* aimed specifically at screenwriters, that seeks to break down many of Aristotle's brilliant concepts and demonstrate how his techniques of dramatic story structure are still used in modern movies. I know how hard it is to read the *Poetics* in its entirety. There's that translation-from-ancient-Greek issue, not to mention the fact that many of the plays Aristotle refers to have vanished or are rarely performed. Some of the conventions he describes have no bearing in today's cinematic world, including talk of "dithyrambs" and other outmoded forms of dramatic writing. However, the *Poetics* is still useful to screenwriters because Aristotle explained why well-structured dramatic works affected audiences the way they did. He analyzed plot devices, character, and everything you'd find in a Hollywood story coverage sheet today. In fact, I think it's safe to say that Aristotle, besides being the greatest mind in Western civilization, was the world's first movie story analyst!

Aristotle's examination of plays such as *Oedipus Rex* demonstrates timeless universal truths about dramatic storytelling. In analyzing great movies like *Rocky* and *American Beauty*, I discovered that they follow Aristotelian story structure, which is not to say they simply follow a bunch of rules. On the contrary, in these works, the art of storytelling is alive and fresh, and perhaps that is why they emerged like beacons from the cluttered marketplace. In each great movie I analyze, the screenwriters and directors have understood how audiences respond to drama, which is what the *Poetics* is all about. This understanding is what makes classic films timeless and awe-inspiring.

The passages from the *Poetics* I cite in the subsequent chapters contain the soundest principles of screenwriting technique ever articulated. What parenthetical emphasis I have added or any rearranging I have done I felt was necessary for the sake of presenting Aristotle's thoughts on dramatic structure as clearly and simply as he intended. You will notice that throughout most of the book, I demonstrate these principles by citing actual movies rather than screenplays. I feel that screenwriters must first understand how drama works in great movies on *screen* before they can make it happen on paper.

A word about the semantics of the *Poetics* needs mentioning. When Aristotle says "tragedy," he means "serious drama," so whenever you see "tragedy" throughout the book (notably in the *Poetics* excerpts), it means just that—not necessarily "tragic drama," in the conventional sense modern viewers hold. In Aristotle's day, there was a hard-core split between tragedy (drama) and comedy. Tragedy was about serious issues—the "tragic deed" and higher-level personages falling from grace. Comedy, about buffoons and lower-level personages that were not to be taken seriously, amounted to a sort of "vaudeville." Aristotle informs us that the sadder dramatic works are indeed the most potent kind, a notion that came to define classical "tragedy," as championed by Shakespeare with works such as *Hamlet* and *King Lear*. But all of the principles about tragedy laid out in the *Poetics* apply to most movies today, even comedies like *Galaxy Quest*.

And now the moment we've all been waiting for . . . storytelling secrets from the greatest mind in Western civilization.

The Action-Idea

Orestes is made to say himself what the poet rather than the story demands.

"Say what the story demands" is a concept that should be pasted on every screenwriter's wall. It's probably *the* pearl of wisdom from *The Poetics*, which Aristotle gets at in the above passage. Here, he's referring to the Greek tragedy *Iphigenia in Tauris*, a play that he feels is flawed because the author (Euripides) made the mistake of letting his own agenda seep into the story rather than having every plot incident come together to create a tight unified structure. In fact, the ability to plot well or create strong story structures is not a minor talent, and according to Aristotle it comes with maturity:

... beginners succeed earlier with the Diction and Characters than with the construction of a story.

According to Aristotle, the ability to plot, or to create a powerful structure, is the most important aspect of writing. Good writers serve their stories; bad writers serve their own agendas. By the end of this book, you'll understand why it's important to say what the story demands. You'll be able to judge if you're doing so, and if not, how to fix it! And to help you in this quest, I want to introduce you to a tool that I call the ACTION-IDEA.

I'm going to refer to this ACTION-IDEA throughout the rest of the book because it represents the essence of Aristotle's *Poetics*. Screenwriters (and directors) must instill their story's ACTION-IDEA, or "mission statement," into an audience to create emotions in them. The ACTION-IDEA is really the foundation of the entire screenplay. A good movie expands an ACTION-IDEA into a full-length story, without losing the essence of the simple idea upon which it is based. While dramatic movies seek to convey a truth about the human condition, it is through the ACTION-IDEA that the screenwriter's particular worldview is best conveyed.

That said, let me now explain more fully what I mean by ACTION-IDEA. Aristotle teaches us to think of AC-TION as the IDEA of a story. In fact, he says that action is more important than people; that is, characters. Aristotle is fanatical about the need for our stories to be about action, about action that is larger than life itself and greater than the persons who partake in it. Think about all the people who say they're going to do a million things, but in the end, you judge them by what they actually accomplish. That's why we screenwriters build a dramatic story on a single action. The hero in a dramatic story is whoever takes the *lead* in that action. For example, *Jaws* is an idea about a man trying to stop a killer shark. Chief Brody takes the lead in the action of trying to stop the killer shark. But notice that the IDEA for *Jaws* is an ACTION upon which the entire story is built. We could reduce the ACTION even further to read, "stopping a killer shark," an ACTION that is greater than any of the characters in the story, even Chief Brody.

Your ACTION-IDEA should be able to move listeners who merely hear it just as they would be moved if they saw an entire movie made from your screenplay. It takes a full-length movie to bring an audience to "catharsis," or profound emotional release, but the ACTION-IDEA should be able to evoke a little bit of that same deep feeling on its own. So, if your ACTION-IDEA must do all this work, it must be a simple summary of a story, strong enough so that when it's expanded into a complete screenplay, it will hold and move an audience. Let's now give the ACTION-IDEA a try.

Say we want to write about someone who likes cars. That's not an ACTION-IDEA. Okay, how about someone who not only likes cars but who likes them so much that he *steals* them. "Steals" is better than "likes" because "steals" refers to an action, whereas "likes" refers to a state of mind. But the idea of a hero who merely *steals* cars isn't *in and of itself* capable of moving an audience to a catharsis. It needs something. So, a better example of an ACTION-IDEA would read something like:

THE JOE SCHMO STORY—JOE SCHMO steals cars to help kids in his neighborhood go to college, but he eventually decides he's setting a bad example, so he goes to college himself so that someday he

can get a real job and earn the money to put his kids
through school. At college he struggles to transcend his
50 I.Q., but instead of bribing teachers to pass his classes,
he decides to pass on his own merits, setting the ultimate
example for his kids.

Bravo! We did it. We created an ACTION-IDEA suitable for building into a full-length film. And notice that the finishing touch was adding the fact that Joe Schmo, the *agent* of the action, got to make a *moral* choice, two important Aristotelian concepts. Admit it, with Joe's decision to pass college on his own merits to set an example, you can't help but *feel* for him. And that's what it's all about, getting the audience to feel and to connect with your characters.

Of course, you might get cute and ask, "If the ACTION-IDEA is capable *in and of itself* of doing emotional work on an audience, why make them sit through a two-hour movie?" The answer could be, "What else are we going to do on Saturday nights?" The real answer is that undergoing catharsis through a full-length story is a richer experience than listening to the mere summation of a story in a few sentences.

According to Aristotle, catharsis (which literally translates to "emotional purging") is the whole point of dramatic storytelling, and it's what every single story event is working to achieve in the audience. Your movie should take the audience on an emotional and psychological journey—that is what they pay for. A good movie reveals poignant truths of the human experience in either a small or big way, depending on the kind of movie it is.

Just hearing a good ACTION-IDEA can impart a small feeling of catharsis, but the bigger drawn-out one experienced during a complete movie is more cleansing for the human psyche, and even therapeutic. Bear in mind, a secret to understanding catharsis is that it doesn't happen at the end of watching a movie, but builds throughout the entire story and *climaxes* at the end, giving the audience a final release.

A well-crafted story is needed to make an ACTION-IDEA cathartic. Our task is to take our simple ACTION-IDEA and develop it into a full-length screenplay, without abandoning the essence of the original idea. So now, all that's left is for me to lead you to the master who can point the way. The task is easier than you think.

1.

Let's Start at the Very Beginning, Middle, and End

. . . a whole is that which has beginning, middle, and end.

This quote from the *Poetics* has led to the common misconception held by many screenwriters that the *Poetics* preaches a three-act structure as the be-all, end-all template for a dramatic story. In fact, Aristotle never stipulates three acts, but he does talk about two distinct movements in a dramatic story, the "complication" and the "denouement":

> Every tragedy [dramatic story] is in part Complication and in part Denouement; the incidents before the opening scene, and . . . also of those within the play, forming the Complication; and the rest the Denouement. By Complication I mean all from the beginning of the story to the point just before the change in the hero's fortunes; by Denouement, all from the beginning of the change to the end.

In cinematic terms, the complication includes everything that happens in the back story that pertains to the plot, and continues through the opening of the movie until right before the change in the hero's fortune occurs. That said, how does beginning, middle, and end apply to story structure? Let's go to the actual excerpt:

> Tragedy is an imitation of an action that is whole and complete in itself and of some magnitude . . . a whole is that which has *beginning, middle, and end.* * A beginning is that which is not itself necessarily after anything else, and which has naturally something else after it; an end is that which is naturally after something itself, either as its necessary or usual consequent, and with nothing else after it; and a middle, that which is by nature after one thing and has also another after it. A well-constructed Plot, therefore, cannot either begin or end at any point one likes; beginning and end in it must be of the kind just described.

In other words, it is the plot action that has a beginning, middle, and end. The plot's beginning "is not *necessarily* after anything else"; that is, the beginning of the plot action cannot be caused by something outside it. It starts up by itself. It's a self-initiated action, a virtual "big bang" that sets the entire plot in motion, that can be committed by either the protagonist or antagonist, and that is an act of pure will. For example, in *The Godfather,* Sollozzo tries to kill the Don so

---

*Emphasis added. All such emphasis in italics in the excerpts has been added by the author throughout the book, unless otherwise noted.

that he can usher in drugs, an action that sets the entire plot in motion. But this action was only necessary from his point of view. In *Dead Poets Society,* Mr. Keating shows his students old photos of now deceased students and tells them "seize the day," urging them to take action before it is too late and to follow their dreams. Nothing in the plot has caused Keating to challenge his students in this way. Because this kind of inciting incident is not caused by anything else in the plot, yet sets the entire plot in motion, I call it a "first cause" of action. These inciting incidents in *The Godfather* and *Dead Poets Society* are perfect examples of first causes of action.

It is important to understand that the first cause of action must occur *after* the movie begins, *not* in the back story. But the first cause of action *must* happen *early* in the movie, because it must be solely responsible for setting off the chain of events that drive the plot. To give writers some space to work with before the first cause of action kicks the plot off, Aristotle offers us a tool called the "prologue." A prologue connects the back-story part of the complication (e.g., what happened to the hero before we meet him) to the "front story" (story after the movie starts) and otherwise sets the stage before the first cause of action happens. In *The Godfather*, the wedding sequence creates atmosphere, introduces characters, and provides a tranquil lead-up to the gunning down of the Don. The nanosecond this first cause of action occurs, we're smack in the "middle" of the plot, as defined by Aristotle. This middle is completely driven by the first cause of action and *naturally* follows after it in a cause-and-effect manner. And just as the first cause of action is a dynamic jolt of energy that drives the middle of the story, it builds to create a "second cause of action" which is also the final plot point of the story, and brings us into the denouement, or "end" movement.

For example, in *The Godfather*, the middle of the plot terminates when Michael becomes Godfather. This change in his fortune marks the beginning of the denouement, during which Michael has enemies from *within* his family killed. The denouement continues until the last frame of the movie; it's not just a final punctuation; it's an entire final movement. It takes time. And like the middle, it *naturally* unfolds in a cause-and-effect way. But Aristotle is very specific about what must happen in this denouement and warns us not to screw it up:

> There are many dramatists who, after a good Complication, fail in the Denouement. But it is necessary for both points of construction to be always duly mastered.

In the denouement, all the plot action that got "wound up" in the middle unravels. For example, in *The Godfather*, the denouement begins with the change in Michael's fortune, which is the jolt that causes the unraveling. But what really unravels in this denouement? Well, since Aristotle believed dramatists must depict not merely life but the *moral* life of a hero, what gets wound up and unravels in the end must concern the hero's moral conflict that developed during the story's middle. So what was Michael's moral conflict in *The*

Godfather? He had sworn off his family's mafia business because it was criminal and unacceptable, but it became equally unacceptable *not* to get involved and in fact became necessary, once his father was shot. When, in the denouement, Michael has Tessio and Carlos killed, his moral dilemma is resolved: He has embraced his fate as the Godfather.

It is through the resolution of the hero's moral conflict in the denouement that the "theme" of the movie is stated. The theme reveals a truth about the human condition that has been demonstrated by the story's action. *The Godfather* makes the following thematic statement: "Sometimes you must sacrifice yourself and your beliefs in order to do what's best for your family." Michael dreamed of having a life different from his father's, but his commitment to his family draws him into the world he wished to escape.

Finally, the denouement itself must come to an end. According to Aristotle, once the plot action has concluded, the audience must know this unequivocally:

> An end is that which is naturally after something itself, either as its necessary or usual consequent, and with nothing else after it.

To summarize, let's touch on the key points of what constitutes a "beginning, middle, and end." The **beginning** of the plot action occurs soon after the movie starts with a "first cause of action," which is a self-initiated, inciting incident that is a pure act of will—nothing causes it, or makes it necessary. This action heralds the **middle** of the plot action, which moves forward through cause and effect, realizing the first movement of the drama, or "complication." The middle, which naturally springs from the first cause of action, drives the story until right before the change in the hero's fortune. This change is the "second cause of action," which begins the denouement, or **end** movement. In the denouement the plot action that got wound up in the complication and that centers on the moral conflict of the hero unravels. As a result, the conflict resolves and truth is gained, wherein lies the theme of the story. When the story concludes, the audience must know for certain that it has and that the plot action will not continue. All of these major points of dramatic story construction can be clearly delineated in a simple ACTION-IDEA as demonstrated here:

THE GODFATHER—After an attempt on DON CORLEONE's life, MICHAEL, who had forsaken the family Mafia business, kills SOLLOZZO and POLICE CAPTAIN MCCLUSKEY to save his family, then takes over the family business, kills all his rivals, soon rises to the top of the American Mafia, and becomes the new Godfather. He then kills all the enemies he has *inside* his family. His fate as Godfather is sealed.

Expressed properly, a strong ACTION-IDEA—with a beginning, middle, and end, a complication and a denouement—is the best springboard for writing a screenplay.

2.

Why You Want Your Movie to Be a Bomb!

A tragedy, then, is the imitation of an action that is serious, has magnitude, and is complete in itself.

Care must be taken not to misread the eloquent but unfamiliar language of the *Poetics*. If you quickly read, "A tragedy is an imitation of a serious action, one having magnitude," you might say to yourself, "Yeah, so what else is new?" But then you might look again at this sentence and say, "Wait a minute . . . an 'imitation' of a serious action? What is Aristotle talking about?"

Good question, because you'll see the word "imitation" used throughout the *Poetics*. For the answer, we need to slow down and deconstruct Aristotle's sentence a bit. We've already discussed that "tragedy" means all serious drama, so let's jump to a tougher concept, that drama is "an imitation of a serious action." The stumbling block for a screenwriter attempting to use this concept might be to think "imitation" means a direct copy of something. Therefore, an "imitation of serious action" could make him think he's supposed to mimic serious events as they might "really" have happened. Remember the scene in *The Player* when a Hollywood suit thinks he can copy newspaper events as they are, put them directly on screen, and make a good story? Well, that's the wrong way to go about dramatic writing. Any seasoned screenwriter or development exec will tell you that "reality" is often quite boring and not dramatic enough to produce the kind of engagement and emotional response your audience is looking for.

What Aristotle means by "imitation" is something quite different from just copying real-life events. For him, the word "imitation" refers to how the "imitative arts" such as painting, music, and drama really work. These arts re-create reality but must be deliberately ordered and shape the resulting make-believe world to induce emotion in their audiences. Viewers are going to allow your story to have a fair amount of "artifice" in its structure and design as long as it moves them. In fact, the action must "imitate" so effectively that the audience responds "imitatively" as well, as if to real events, their brains aroused to a state of action.

Perhaps Alfred Hitchcock said it best when he claimed that if a bomb under a table suddenly explodes out of nowhere in a movie, it's not a great movie. That is, the audience needs to know *beforehand* that a bomb is under the table and that it is *about* to explode. This information actually puts their brains into a state of action by raising the tense dramatic question, "*When* is the bomb going to explode?" That the characters themselves are unaware of the bomb engages the audience's attention and compels them to heightened mental participation in the story action.

But we need to know how to make more than just one

scene work, more than how to have just one bomb explode under a table. We need a way for all the action in our story to be unified and to develop into "one big idea," one single connected story. The best way to do this is not by raising a bunch of little questions, but by raising, developing, and answering one central dramatic question in the audience's brain. So, let's see how *Dead Poets Society* planted its bomb.

In this movie, events are chosen and shaped to raise the question, "Will the boys learn from Keating to live life to the fullest and follow their dreams, or will the soulless schoolmasters win and turn the boys into lifeless drones?" This question takes us all the way through the story. It keeps the audience interested in the outcome and contributes to its ability to experience the "imitation" of emotions it would feel if threatened by a real soulless schoolmaster. In fact, it's a good idea to state the ACTION-IDEA in a way that *implies* a central dramatic question:

DEAD POETS SOCIETY—Professor KEATING inspires young students to live for their dreams, which causes them to start a poetry society. One boy, NEIL, defies his FATHER and takes up acting, then kills himself when he's transferred to military school, which causes KEATING to get fired. The boys stand on their desks and honor their teacher as he exits.

The whole design of *Dead Poets Society* raises the central dramatic question beautifully, using a very strong first cause

IMMPERMANANCE
Lot This relative life is fleeting.

of action. When Keating takes his students to look at 100-year-old photos of deceased students and conveys his message to them, "Carpe diem" (seize the day)—take action now to live life to the fullest—the "bomb" is clearly planted under the table. The audience is hooked as it begins ticking . . .

All the scenes that follow are connected to this cause of action, through what Aristotle refers to as "probable" or "necessary" incidents that help move the plot along and develop the central dramatic question. Each scene arises from the previous scene in a way that plays to the audience's mental participation and focus, and dramatic "imitation" of action succeeds in provoking an emotional response. Keating doesn't just say words to inspire the boys, he makes them rip pages out of books and stand on their desks to read Whitman (in "real" life, an inspirational teacher might not be quite so dramatic). These events eventually spur the boys to form their own Dead Poets Society. They hide out in the woods, where they write and read poetry aloud, bang drums, play saxophones, dance in circles, paint their faces, and invite girls to read poetry. The action develops as Knox tries to date Christine and gets beaten up by her boyfriend, and Todd throws his desk set off the roof, in symbolic defiance of convention and orderliness (and his parents).

As the story moves on, the bomb ticks louder. The serious magnitude of the action in *Dead Poets Society* builds to a peak when Neil gets the lead in the school play, setting his sights on an acting career. But Neil's father is going to make sure his son becomes a soulless master of the universe and pulls him out of school, enrolling him into a military academy. Because he sees no other way out of his situation, Neil shoots himself. The bomb has exploded!

At this point the audience is asking, "Now what's going to happen to Keating and the boys?" Even though the action has now gained serious magnitude, the central dramatic question is still hanging. When the boys are forced to play Judas and blow the whistle on Keating (blaming him for causing Neil's suicide), the glorious answer is prepared: The boys stand on their desks to honor the fired Keating, despite the old schoolmaster's threat to expel them. This final action is one that might never happen in "real" life, but it sure is a great "imitation" of life that induces deep, cathartic emotions in the audience. And it brings home the boys'—and the audience's—emotional journey.

CATHARSIS .

Write your screenplays to raise, develop, and answer one central dramatic question so that your reader or audience will stay hooked. Hopefully when your screenplay is covered, the bomb of your central dramatic question will be heard ticking in the story analyst's head as well. And someday that ticking will turn into the ringing of a cash register when you finally sell your script. How's that for a serious action with magnitude!

3.

The Subject Is an Action . . .
Not a Person

. . . the story, as an imitation of action, must represent one action.

Aristotle believed that a dramatic story must have unity if it's going to move an audience and bring it to catharsis. He also knew that dramatic writers were often fooled into thinking that because they used one hero throughout an entire story, this alone unified their plots. Screenwriters make the same mistake today. But the appearance of Hercules in every frame of a movie *about* Hercules, according to Aristotle in no way ensures dramatic unity:

> The Unity of a Plot does not consist, as some suppose, in its having one man as its subject. An infinity of things befall that one man, some of which it is impossible to reduce to unity; and in like manner there are many actions of one man which cannot be made to form one action. One sees, therefore, the mistake of all the poets who have written . . . similar poems; they suppose that, because Heracles was one man, the story also of Heracles must be one story.

Aristotle insists that in a unified dramatic story the subject is an action, not a person. By presenting one strong unified action from a hero's life, you depict the hero. For example, if on a job interview, a potential employer asks you to tell him about something that depicts "you," you'd tell him about something significant you'd accomplished. This would "sum you up" better than telling him a million anecdotes about what your personality is like. Screenwriting works the same way: You write a single unified action as a "through line," which becomes the story's subject. Then a hero takes the *lead* in that action, which has a "oneness" and connectivity so clear that Aristotle compares it to a statue:

> In the other imitative arts [like sculpture] one imitation
> is always of one thing, so in poetry the story, as an imitation of
> action, must represent one action, a complete whole.

When we see a statue of a man, it's easy to see what the one whole thing is . . . a statue. That's how tight and unified a story's action must be. But while a statue is frozen, a story moves through time, so for action to be unified and form a "whole," its incidents must have what Aristotle termed a *probable* or *necessary* cause-and-effect connection:

> In writing an *Odyssey*, he did not make the poem cover
> all that ever befell his hero—it befell him, for instance, to
> get wounded on Parnassus and also to feign madness at
> the time of the call to arms, but the two incidents had

no probable or necessary connexion with one another—
instead of doing that, he took an action with a Unity of
the kind we are describing as the subject of the *Odyssey*,
as also of the *Iliad*.

Homer chose for the "subject" of *The Odyssey* an action
in which each incident follows the previous one in a necessary or probable way and at the same time causes the story
to go forward. Such cause-and-effect linkage makes the story's
action coherent in the same way a statue's parts fit together to
form one image. However, there are key differences between
probable cause-and-effect incidents and necessary ones.

Incidents of necessity *always* happen after a given cause
of action and propel the story forward. For example, if you
came home and found your house broken into and robbed
you would always call the police; calling the police is an
action that *necessarily* follows the incident of discovering
your house robbed. As we discussed previously, *The Godfather*'s inciting incident is Sollozzo having the Don shot,
which causes Michael to kill Sollozzo and Captain Mc-
Cluskey. Sollozzo's action *causes* or makes it *necessary* for
Michael to kill Sollozzo and McCluskey in the restaurant.

Probable dramatic incidents also cause the story to go
forward but are only *likely* to happen. They aren't incidents
of dramatic necessity, in terms of how the characters view
their own actions. For example, in *Rocky* it makes sense that
after Rocky gets a shot at the boxing crown, Mickey begs
him to be his manager, *but this didn't have to happen*. How-

ever, notice that this *probable* incident causes the story action to go forward: Mickey trains Rocky, which *causes* him to last 15 rounds. Rocky taking Mickey on also helps the audience like Rocky, and since Rocky is our hero, we have to like him in order to care about what happens to him. Rocky's relationship with Adrienne is similarly constructed, in that their courtship is a sequence of probable events.

Because *Rocky* uses more probable incidents than necessary ones its chain of cause-and-effect events feels looser than *The Godfather*'s, but it's still a tight, unified plot. Let's take a look at its ACTION-IDEA.

ROCKY—ROCKY desires to be more than a bum from the neighborhood and tries to accomplish this in many ways. He gets offered a chance to fight the champ APOLLO CREED, and decides he only wants to last fifteen rounds to prove he's not a bum. He trains for the match and does last fifteen rounds.

The boxing match becomes an important goal for Rocky—if he wins, he proves he's more than a bum, but everything that happens in the plot is about him becoming more than a bum (his ultimate goal).

Rocky not only has a strong plot, but it also develops a great character, fulfilling two essential criteria for moving an audience. A tight plot need not be like a predictable row of dominoes knocking each other down. It's more important that the incidents that form the plot have either a probable or necessary relationship to each other and cause the story to move forward. Rocky dating Adrienne, Paulie putting ads on Rocky's robe, Mickey training him—all of these incidents are probable and cause Rocky to grow, and draw him closer to his change in fortune. In fact, that's what a unified action does: It depicts the transformation of a hero's fortune, and the boxing match with Apollo Creed is the supreme way it finally happens for Rocky.

Aristotle tells us that the plot should be so tight that if you took away any one incident, the whole would literally collapse:

> [The plot should have] its several incidents so closely connected that the transposal or withdrawal of any one of them will disjoin and dislocate the whole. For that which makes no perceptible difference by its presence or absence is no real part of the whole.

There is another important passage of the *Poetics* that pertains to developing tight, unified dramatic action:

> From what we have said it will be seen that the poet's function is to describe, not the thing that has happened, but a kind of thing that might happen i.e. *what is possible* [or like life] as being probable or necessary.

Here, Aristotle reminds us that making a plot action unified requires not only that the *individual* incidents be connected

through probable or necessary cause and effect. He insists
that the *entire chain of plot events* must form a story that
seems "probable" or "necessary."

For example, the incidents of *The Godfather* and *Rocky*
have an overall, archetypal logic to how they are connected.
The events that unfold give the appearance that they would
always happen in the story world they represent, or at least
they would probably happen. That's because good dramatic
stories depict universals of human lives and actions. For
example, in *The Godfather*, given the kind of man Michael
Corleone is, it makes sense that he reacts in the way that he
does; hence the events that occur in *The Godfather* would
"always" or "necessarily" happen in that story world. Or at
least they would "probably" happen. But we all know real
life doesn't happen in a tight, unified cause-and-effect manner the way movie action happens. However, movie stories
must present a believable world based on an imaginary chain
of events. This is the paradox of screenwriting.

The lesson Aristotle teaches us is this: Make your
ACTION-IDEA the driving force behind every scene and
the subject of your story. Make your main character take the
lead in such a tight unified plot action, which is both logical
and compelling, and you'll "make" the kind of script Hollywood movie executives will definitely notice. And who
knows! Maybe your screenplay will be an offer Hollywood
can't refuse. Which means you can break in *without* having
to sever any horses' heads, because like statues and story
action, Hollywood folk like their horses to remain unified.

4.

Forget Sub-plotting—
the Best Plots Have
One-Track Minds

The perfect Plot, accordingly, must have a single, and not (as some tell us) a double issue.

Aristotle's *Poetics* can't teach you to write all kinds of screenplay plots, just the ones that work. As we have seen, effective plots are unified—they have a single, not a double, as Aristotle puts it, "issue." That is to say: no sub-plots. Aristotle argued way back when that using sub-plots was a bad technique in dramatic writing, and it's *still* a bad technique in screenwriting. While it's easy to see how *The Godfather* has a "single issue" plot (the war waged on the Corleones), you could be fooled into thinking that *American Beauty* has many "issues," or sub-plots. It doesn't. It contains a single issue, one unified action, and no sub-plots. All the action, no matter how many characters are running around performing "sub-actions," is related through either probable or necessary cause and effect. This is important, because as Aristotle warns us in this famous passage:

>   Episodic [plots] are the worst. I call a Plot episodic
>   when there is neither probability nor necessity [causality]
>   in the sequence of its episodes.

The "single issue" action that ties *American Beauty* together is simply this: The perception of beauty and the effect
it has on people's lives is an action in which all the characters in their own way participate. Ricky Fitz comments on
this "single issue" when he shows Janey a floating bag and
recounts how this image prompted him to realize that there
is so much beauty in the world, he feels as though his heart
may burst. This single issue, the perception of beauty, with
the longing and anguish it entails, becomes the story's "one-
track mind." All the characters are driven by this mindset.
Lester chases Angela, Janey goes for Ricky, Angela wants
Lester, Lester's wife Carol hooks up with Buddy, and Colonel Fitz kisses Lester. Obviously, a unified chain of events.

For the record, there is some separate cause and effect
in the sub-actions of the secondary characters going on, but
these sub-actions converge to make the story ONE COM-
PLETE ACTION. All the action connects to Lester, the
hero who takes the *lead*. For a demonstration of how this
works, let's first review its ACTION-IDEA:

AMERICAN BEAUTY—LESTER, a middle-
aged man, whose wife and daughter think he's a
loser, has lost all desire for life. LESTER gets infatuated
with sixteen-year-old ANGELA, causing him to get fired,

smoke pot, and work out. He catches the eye of his neighbor COLONEL FITZ, a Neo-Nazi homophobe. After rejecting a sexual advance from the COLONEL, LESTER almost has sex with ANGELA but learns she's a virgin, decides not to have sex with her, and regains his dignity. Then COLONEL FITZ murders him, and in his dying moments Lester realizes the beauty of just being alive.

American Beauty uses information shown in the sub-actions of the plot to feed the audience information about what Lester's going through and why. Aristotle teaches us that while an audience can automatically "get" the setup (a man in mid-life crisis chasing a teenage girl), there are details about this action that an audience *can't* assume. The audience needs to derive information about the specifics of what's causing Lester's action, and this information comes from other characters. As Aristotle tells us:

A tragedy, then, is the imitation of an action that is serious, has magnitude, and is complete in itself.

In other words, whatever information isn't universal (that which an audience can "get" automatically) must be able to be deduced from the story world *through events in that story world*, even if this information comes through sub-actions. For example, a big *cause* of Lester's infatuation with Angela is the fact that his marriage has died. But what was the nature of this love Lester lost, which is *causing* his crisis? The audience can't know what he lost; this cause of the action must be fed to them. This is done through Janey and Ricky, their young innocent love providing a model of what Lester once had. Ricky's personality, his very "being" provides the audience with information that helps it imagine the youthful spirit Lester had, that's gone. The details relating to what *causes* Lester's mid-life crisis, like what he's lost, must be telegraphed to the audience through minor scenes, such as Lester buying dope from Ricky as he fondly remembers his teenage years, when he flipped burgers all summer in order to buy an eight-track player. The actual incidents of the story must convey the nature of what's "causing" the character's actions: You have to "show it" not just tell it.

To further underscore how *American Beauty*'s plot has a one-track mind, consider how all the characters "share" in Lester's murder: Carol brings home a gun and charges into the house, ranting about "not being a victim," as if she were whipping herself into a frenzy in order to kill Lester. Then she discovers his body and guiltily hides her gun. Janey and Ricky were in the house and had previously talked about killing Lester. And Angela, who is looking into the bathroom mirror when she hears the shot, was "involved" by mere virtue of her beauty, which caused Lester's reawakening and set off the chain of events that eventually leads to his death. Finally, there is the colonel, who actually kills Lester. So every character either contemplated Lester's murder or had some causal relationship to it. This tragic deed *resolves* all the action in the story and makes it ONE COMPLETE ACTION in a very concrete way.

American Beauty has no sub-plots, only sub-actions driven by a single issue and thereby connected to the hero's action, all of it ultimately forming ONE COMPLETE ACTION, which is neatly resolved by the murder of the hero at the end.

Abandon the concept of sub-plots, structure your screenplay as well as *American Beauty* is structured, and you may end up with a cinematic beauty, and maybe even an Oscar.

5.

Plot Is Soul

The first essential, the life and soul, so to speak, of Tragedy is the Plot; and that the Characters come second—compare the parallel in painting, where the most beautiful colours laid on without order [unity] will not give one the same pleasure as a simple black-and-white sketch of a portrait.

Now that we know that plot action must be unified, I want to turn you on to a core aspect of what is really behind unified plot action. Until now, you might have thought that plot-driven movies and character-driven movies are mutually exclusive. But Aristotle teaches how plot and character work together way beyond just the technical logic of necessary and probable incidents. He tells us why we bother to link action so tightly. When Aristotle insists that random colors won't give a spectator as much pleasure as a simple black-and-white sketch of a portrait, he's not choosing his metaphors lightly. He implies that the unity of a plot through causally related incidents forms the image of a human being! The key is to have the plot action connected to the deep desiring soul of your hero. This is what he means in the *Poetics* quote above, which I like to paraphrase down to "plot is soul." When a strong desire of a hero relates to all of the action, then the plot can depict a simple "portrait" of the hero.

The action of *Rocky* is connected to Rocky's desire to make more of his life. He dates Adrienne, argues with Mickey, and attempts to save a twelve-year-old girl from the streets. Then he learns Apollo wants to fight him, and Mickey trains him for the match. Rocky confesses to Adrienne that he can't win the fight, but only wants to last fifteen rounds so that he'll know he isn't just another bum from the neighborhood. With this great line of dialog and in a stroke of screenwriting genius, the story's action is galvanized and its dramatic unity becomes crystal clear, because the hero's desire has been stated. It's important for the audience to understand the *emotional* meaning of the action for the hero, which, to be moving, must be connected to a strong, single desire of the hero's soul. In fact, the emotional experience the audience can get from a movie will be akin to the hero's emotional experience, a good rule of thumb for the screenwriter.

In *Rocky*, when the movie finally cuts to the boxing ring for the final action sequence, the finale is completely charged by the movie's ACTON-IDEA. Every punch Rocky throws and receives is connected to every story incident that preceded it and is emotionally linked to his desire to become somebody. Clearly, *Rocky* derives its soul from its plot and not from its spectacle (the visuals of the fight). And that is what makes it a cinematic masterpiece.

6.

The Ends Are Always in the Means of the Plot

So that it is the action in it, i.e. its Fable or Plot, that is the end and purpose of the tragedy; and the end is everywhere the chief thing.

Aristotle calls the plot the story's "end" and purpose, because to him, "plot is soul" and it's the plot structure that arouses emotions from the audience. When Aristotle uses a term like "end" to describe plot, he's saying that the ACTION-IDEA, or plot, must always be in your mind's eye when you are writing scenes. In other words, writing a plot is more than just stitching scenes together. For example, say I wanted to build a tree house. The visual image of the tree house would be my "end" or finished product, and everything to build this house would be a *means* to this end. In all the activity of cutting down trees and hammering wood together, I would be thinking about the final product of the house. This image would serve as a point of focus guiding the activity.

Plotting a script requires the same kind of focus from a writer. For an example of this, let's examine *The Breakfast Club*, starting with its ACTION-IDEA:

THE BREAKFAST CLUB—Five stereotypical high school students, a BRAIN, an ATHLETE, a BASKET CASE, a PRINCESS, and a HOODLUM, are sent to Saturday detention. After initial tension and arguing they open up to each other and discover each has similar alienations, problems with parents, and difficulty living up to their stereotype. This day changes each of them, causing them to realize that they are not that different from each other.

The Breakfast Club's ACTION-IDEA is in all the scenes of the movie. Take the scene where Claire (the princess) talks about how her parents use her as a pawn in their marital fights. This hits a nerve with the hoodlum, who asks questions about Claire's parents because he has problems with his own. Eventually, each student confesses to similar distresses with their families and friends, which these supposedly diverse detention victims are all experiencing. This scene *contains* the plot because you can literally sense the ACTION-IDEA within it. As the kids open up to each other a theme emerges, that of their shared feelings of alienation. In every molecule of the story you can sense the simple ACTION-IDEA because the plot is evoked in every scene.

A simple plot expressed as an ACTION-IDEA will galvanize your screenwriting, the way imaging your finished tree house will inspire you as you saw and chop wood. It's been said that the "the whole is greater than the sum of its parts." Aristotle would agree, but he would remind us that "the whole is always *in* each of the parts."

7.

Why Is My Beautiful Plot Growing a Hand Out of Its Head?

[story should have] all the organic unity of a living creature.

If you were unfortunate enough to be targeted for termination, as Sarah Conner was in *The Terminator*, the Terminator would find you, rip your heart out, and toss it on the ground. Your poor heart would begin to decompose because it would no longer be part of your body. It needs to be in your body to remain alive, and plays a vital role in *keeping* your body alive as well.

Similarly, when Aristotle states that a plot is a living creature with "no extraneous organs," he means that scenes have no power but in how they are organized to make a living plot. Scenes aren't alive only as they happen on the screen; they *stay* alive in the audience's psyche as the plot builds there. The audience must always be focusing on a simple ACTION-IDEA of the plot throughout every story event.

Dramatic story works very much like a pop song. When a singer sings a song with the refrain, "There goes my baby," no matter how many minutes the song drags on, we are consistently focusing on the simple plot of the song, that the singer lost his girl. Because the song's plot stays simple, we can concentrate on the *emotional* impact it's supposed to have on us.

The same goes with movie stories. Scenes are organs that are like song "choruses": They don't add key plot incidents, but they do add emotional depth, meaning, and *magnitude*. They make the reality of the simple plot seem more real and terrifying, as is the case in *The Terminator*.

The "organs," or scenes, work together to give "life" to a plot, which means you don't add scenes to make the ACTION-IDEA have more and more plot lines, you add scenes to make the ACTION-IDEA have more emotional impact on the audience. To get to the heart of this matter, let's examine *The Terminator*'s ACTION-IDEA:

THE TERMINATOR—A robot from the future is sent back to the present to kill SARAH CONNER because she is destined to give birth to JOHN CONNER, the future savior of the world. REESE from the future comes to help save her, impregnates her, and before he is killed, helps her destroy the TERMINATOR so she can give birth to their son, JOHN CONNER.

A vital "organ" of this plot occurs at the very beginning of the film, when the naked Terminator asks the teenage hoodlum for his clothes, and the teenager responds by stabbing him in the chest, at which point the Terminator doesn't even flinch. In one move, he rips out the heart of the teenager. We immediately see he's not of this world, but is an indestructible killing machine on a mission. This scene has not added any core incidents to the simple ACTION-IDEA of *The Terminator*, but helps it become clearer and deeper, and adds to its power and meaning. This scene enhances the first line of the ACTION-IDEA, "a Terminator from the future is here to kill . . ." The audience will be asking themselves questions . . . What's a "Terminator"? How does he kill, why is he killing, and what does he want? What is so damn important that this incredibly advanced piece of machinery has traveled across time to do this terrible business? The scene where the Terminator rips out the hoodlum's heart develops the story's magnitude. As Aristotle tells us,

> to be beautiful, a living creature, and every whole made up of parts, must not only present a certain order in its arrangement of parts, but also be of a certain definite magnitude.

A plot's power and emotional impact can't grow merely because a character talks about what's going on in the story. The plot's magnitude grows when all the organs or scenes are working together to give life to the simple living plot. The scene where the Terminator rips out the teenager's heart is a violent demonstration of what the Terminator is here to do and how; a vital organ of the living plot that will remain in the audience's brain and be used to develop the story's magnitude and emotional impact on the audience. It accomplishes this without adding anything that needs to be focused on in terms of basic plot line. Just like a heart is always present in a living body, strong scenes that happen in a movie always stay present in the audience's brain and impact everything else that happens.

Keep the plot a simple ACTION-IDEA. Add scenes as organs that develop its emotional impact on the audience, without complicating it. Otherwise, you might add extraneous "organs" or scenes to it, and your plot will grow a hand out of its head, causing your screenplay to be targeted for termination. And that's gotta hurt!

8.

The Four Species of Plot

There are four distinct species of Tragedy . . .
first, the complex Tragedy, which is all Peripety*
[reversal of fortune] and Discovery; second, the
Tragedy of suffering . . . third, the Tragedy of char-
acter . . . The fourth constituent is that of "Specta-
cle," exemplified in The Phorcides, in Prometheus,
and in all the plays with the scene laid in the
nether world.

Aristotle tells us there are four "species" of dramatic story. For us, this breaks down into four different types of dramatic movies.

1. **Complex** (containing a "Reversal of Fortune/Discovery"). Examples of complex plots are *Angel Heart* and *Rosemary's Baby*. These movies are the kind where a plot builds to a moment when the hero's fortune goes from extremely good to extremely bad instantly (or the opposite), based on a discovery or recognition. The recognition involves a switch from extreme ignorance to

---

*Peripety means "the change of the kind described from one state of things within the play to its opposite."

knowledge. This type of plot is Aristotle's favorite, and will be the principal sort of plot that we'll study through-out this book.

It's worth mentioning that Aristotle also describes what he calls the "simple" plot:

> Plots are either simple or complex, since the actions they represent are naturally of this twofold description. The action, proceeding in the way de-fined as one continuous whole I call simple, when the change in the hero's fortunes takes place *without [a reversal of fortune] or Discovery;* and complex, when it involves one or the other, or both.

Clerks is a day in the life of a young convenience store clerk who has to show up to his boring job on his day off and deal with all the irate customers that come in. It's a story that uses the degrading environment of the lower level "slacker"-type jobs to evoke the gloom that America's youth feels toward the coming reality of the work world that awaits them and is a good example of a simple plot.

2. **Tragedy of suffering.** Aristotle teaches us that all good tragedy has suffering, and most good dramatic movies contain a certain amount of intense physical or mental suffering, or both. Some movies contain suffering to such a degree that it would seem as if the suffering were

the very soul of the drama. Ingmar Bergman's work involves so much psychological suffering on the part of the characters (and audience) that his stories could be called "tragedies of suffering." Aristotle might say that in Bergman's work, "suffering is the soul." You might want to check out some of his masterpieces on videotape, works like *Persona*, *Cries and Whispers*, and *Through a Glass Darkly*.

3. **Tragedy of character**. Mike Leigh develops his plots through improvisations with actors. The result is lively character studies that become films like *Naked*, *Career Girls*, and *Secrets and Lies*. These films are more interested in developing the nuances of characterizations and relationships in a loosely plotted way that emphasizes personality and character traits.

4. **Spectacle**. Movies of spectacle are very abundant in today's cinema. The most recent example of such a movie is *Moulin Rouge*. Stanley Kubrick's work also thrives on spectacle and visual atmosphere, especially *2001*. Spectacle refers to the effect of the visuals, that is, the costumes, the scenery, and the actors. This brings to mind the term "mise-en-scène," which is French for "put into a scene." Everything that isn't plot, character, character thought, dialogue, or music track, is mise-en-scène. Remember, spectacle in cinema is *not* just mis-en-scène; sound effects, for example, play a huge role in today's

spectacle-driven cinema. Try and imagine *Jurassic Park* without its brilliant sound effects. This is of interest to screenwriters because they need to have an understanding of the power of the medium they are writing for. Their true medium is the printed page, which is a frightfully reductive way of representing the richest, most lavish medium of all time, the cinema.

That said, it's important to note that all four species of drama can be used together in the same work, as Aristotle reminds us:

> The poet's aim, then, should be to combine every element of interest, if possible, or else the more important and the major part of them. This is now especially necessary owing to the unfair criticism to which the poet is subjected in these days. Just because there have been poets before him strong in the several species of tragedy, the critics now expect the one man to surpass that which was the strong point of each of his predecessors.

Although Aristotle tells us that we might use all four species of drama, he reminds us not to feel obligated to do so. It seems in his day critics were pushing dramatic writers to create plays with *every* kind of pleasure in them, which he thought was undue pressure. Indeed, most mortals are limited in the kinds of stories they can write, but a great example of a movie that *does* use all four species of drama in one film is *Titanic*, a complex drama complete with a reversal of fortune/discovery, spectacle, and suffering.

So you may want to combine all four species of drama in your screenplay. The point is, you should know which one or which combination of them you are using and what kind of dramatic effect you expect to achieve if your screenplay is to survive in the process of Hollywood selection.

9.

What the *Poetics* Says About Epics Like *Lord of the Rings*

There is, however, a difference in the Epic as compared with Tragedy.

According to Aristotle, epic poetry is a genre unto itself and has its own set of lessons for writing. What Aristotle means by "epic" is a narrated story like Homer's *The Iliad*, or *The Odyssey*:

> [The poet] may either (1) speak at one moment in narrative and at another in an assumed character, as Homer does; or (2) one may remain the same throughout, without any such change; or (3) the imitators may represent the whole story dramatically, as though they were actually doing the things described.

In the epic genre, a narrator can switch back and forth between narrating the story ("once upon a time . . .") and using the "first person," which is assuming the voice and point of view of the hero. Or an epic poem can lock into one of these two modes of storytelling all the way through the story. Epic poems can also be acted out dramatically on stage, like tragedy.

Movies often use such techniques from ancient epic poetry; consider how Charles Dickens's novel *Great Expectations* became the David Lean movie of the same name. The movie opens on a shot of the physical novel and we hear a voice-over of Pip, quoting from the novel and telling us how he came to earn the name Pip, and so forth. Lean connects some of the narrative dots by using Pip as a "narrator," combining techniques from both tragedy *and* epic poetry to depict fiction.

In some ways, a movie is a play on the screen (hence the term "screen*play*), but the cinematic medium has huge potential for elaborate and exotic locations, from the bowels of the *Titanic* to the center of a meteor approaching the earth, as in *Armageddon*. In fact, *Armageddon* recalls ancient epic poems, containing multitudes of peoples, great wars, and so on. Part of the reason such works belong to the spoken epic genre is their scale, which made them ludicrous on stage. In short, epic stories didn't lend themselves to the staged dramatic medium and were best if spoken by a narrator.

When we think of "epic" movies, we think of them as grand and sweeping, depicting not so much an everyday reality but an exaggerated reality or fantasy. Even if an epic story tells of a realistic period, it still uses a sweeping mode of presentation. Epic cinematic storytelling might rely on spectacle and visual effects, as well as flashier editing and sound design, but also take place over long periods of time, while dramas work better with compressed time:

> [Epic also differs from tragedy] in its length—which is due to its action having no fixed limit of time, whereas Tragedy endeavours to keep as far as possible within a single circuit of the sun, [24 hours] or something near that.

The best tragedies take place over a single day, as in *Oedipus Rex*. This makes the plot events more intense, giving the change in the hero's fortune the greatest magnitude and the audience the biggest rush. It's easier to make a story "one complete action" and unify all its incidents through causality if the story happens over a day, or close to one day. Some movies compress time to less than twenty-four hours, like *American Graffiti*. But great movies like *The Godfather II* span decades. *The Godfather II* is a fusion of tragic and epic storytelling, with an emphasis on tragic. Also in tragedy, Aristotle tells us to keep "improbable" deeds (unrealistic ones) outside the play (in back story). But this doesn't apply to the epic:

> The Epic, however, affords more opening for the improbable, the chief factor in the marvellous, because in it the agents are not visibly before one. The scene of

the pursuit of Hector would be ridiculous on the stage—
the Greeks halting instead of pursuing him, and Achilles
shaking his head to stop them; but in the poem the ab-
surdity is overlooked.

Epics, because they were narrated, allowed writers to
use any improbable story event they could dream of, because
the "agents" were unseen. Personally, I *still* prefer movies
that make me use my imagination (like *The Blair Witch
Project*) any day over seeing a gazillion special effects thrown
up on the screen to move me. Some of the limitations Aristotle puts on tragic story grew out of his concern about
what could be done on stage versus what could be done
through narration in epics. You can't re-create the Trojan
War on stage the way you can if you have a narrator merely
talk about it.

These limitations have vanished off the face of the earth
for the modern screenwriter. I am convinced that Hollywood
can and will re-create *any* fantastical reality ever penned if
it feels the story will make a great movie and a large profit.
It seems that these days, "the bigger the better."

For a great example of an epic movie, watch *Lord of the
Rings*. Special effects keep getting better, and there is nothing holding producers back from putting great epic masterpieces on the screen. So if your wish is for epics and fantasy,
knock yourself out—Hollywood digs blockbuster epics!
However, be advised, screenwriters who write Hollywood
epics *must* remember that while they may embellish epic

stories in ways that they can't in straight drama, epics and dramas share certain structural requirements:

> The construction of its [epic] stories should clearly be like that of a drama; they should be based on a single action, one that is a complete whole in itself, with a beginning, middle, and end, so as to enable the work to produce its own proper pleasure with all the organic unity of a living creature.

This passage is not merely a refresher on dramatic unity, it lets us know that even a great epic screenplay must have the "dramatic unity of a living creature." This even goes for pulling an epic story from history and dramatizing it for the screen, like *Gone With the Wind*:

> Nor should one suppose that there is anything like them [a story which is a naturally unified action] in our usual histories. A history has to deal not with one action, but with one *period* and all that happened in that to one or more persons, however disconnected the several events may have been. Just as two events may take place at the same time, e.g. the sea-fight off Salamis and the battle with the Carthaginians in Sicily, without converging to the same end, so also of two consecutive events one may sometimes come after the other with no one end as their common issue. Nevertheless most of our epic poets, one may say, ignore the distinction.

Some bad ancient poets had no regard for creating a tight plot when depicting history because they were fooled into thinking that because events had a "unity of time" (were about a historical period and followed one another chronologically), this meant that there was an automatic dramatic unity to those events. In an epic story, you can have multiple story lines but they must all have the same end and resolve the same issue. A recent example is the epic movie *The Mummy Returns*, which has three separate plot lines moving through it, but they all converge on the return of the evil mummy and the subsequent wars and battles caused by him. But remember, this structure differs from more somber, realistic tragic structure.

Epic movies can have filler episodes surrounding the main action for embellishments, but this doesn't stop the story from being mostly about one action:

> Herein, then, to repeat what we have said before, we have a further proof of Homer's marvellous superiority to the rest. He did not attempt to deal even with the Trojan war in its entirety, though it was a whole with a definite beginning and end—through a feeling, apparently, that it was too long a story to be taken in at one view, or if not that, too complicated from the variety of incident in it. As it is, he has singled out one section of the whole; many of the other incidents, however, he brings in as episodes, using the Catalogue of the Ships, for instance, and other episodes to relieve the uniformity

of his narrative. As for the other epic poets, they treat of
one man, or one period; or else of an action which, although one, has a multiplicity of parts in it.

This is probably the best advice for a screenwriter looking
to adapt a book into a screenplay. Aristotle tells us that even
though the Trojan War *naturally* had a beginning and end,
Homer singled out one section of it and made one complete
action of it to depict the war. He added other kinds of scenes
as episodes to break up the monotony, but *The Odyssey* has
a simple ACTION-IDEA as narrative glue. Let's take a look
at Aristotle's definition of *The Odyssey*'s ACTION-IDEA:

A certain man has been abroad many years; Posei-
don is ever on the watch for him, and he is all alone.
Matters at home too have come to this, that his substance
is being wasted and his son's death plotted by suitors to
his wife. Then he arrives there himself after his grievous
sufferings; reveals himself, and falls on his enemies; and
the end is his salvation and their death.

Aristotle informs us that this ACTION-IDEA, which holds
together the massive poem *The Odyssey*, is all that matters
and everything else is filler:

This being all that is proper to the *Odyssey*, everything else in it is episode.

A narrative epic poem allows for more license to throw in episodes not directly related to the ACTION-IDEA, but a simple ACTION-IDEA still holds it all together. So no matter how lavish and grand-sweeping an epic you want to write, remember to consider the fundamentals of dramatic storytelling Aristotle teaches us, in order to get your epic on to the screen.

10.

Destiny Is an Accident
Waiting to Happen

*Even matters of chance seem most marvellous if
there is some appearance of design in them . . . for
incidents like that we think to be not without a
meaning.*

Aristotle's favorite play, *Oedipus Rex*, is about what happens when you try to escape destiny, as Oedipus learns
the hard way. All his efforts to escape his predicted fate
(that he would kill his father and marry his mother) lead
him closer to fulfilling this destiny. Many of the events that
happen in *Oedipus Rex* appear to be chance incidents. However, as the plot unfolds, it becomes clear that these incidents are anything but chance. Oedipus fulfills his destiny
and loses his eyes because he didn't regard the gods' prediction as a serious factor in shaping his life.

He ignored destiny. And while you might think that
modern audiences are too sophisticated to desire the question of destiny to be addressed in movies, think again. Even
chance incidents in *The Blair Witch Project* feed into the
"meaning" of what's going on, namely, that there really *is*
an evil Blair Witch lurking in the dark Maryland woods,

messing with the students. It's not a coincidence that those film students lose their map and find Josh's ear after he disappears. It all starts to form a definitive "meaning," as Aristotle says. It's not a good meaning for those film students, but it's certainly a "marvellous" one for the audience.

The theme of destiny also pops up throughout the hip film *Pulp Fiction*. For example, when the drug dealer shoots and misses Jules, Jules interprets this fluke accident as a sign from God to leave crime. He discusses his newly awakened sense of destiny to Vince as they drive along, but this notion is smashed when their car hits a bump, causing Vince to accidentally shoot and kill Marvin in the backseat. Now events are portrayed as pure accident, almost in response to Jules's earlier encounter with "destiny."

Story incidents that happen by chance are another building block of action, connecting the action through cause and effect the way incidents of necessity and probability do. In *Pulp Fiction*, the appearance of design in the story's chance elements allows Jules to read his luck as destiny, although he also witnesses Marvin's luck run out because of a fluke accident. But perhaps, unlike Oedipus, Jules will go through life with his eyeballs intact, spared from his own violent end, which would come about if he ignored the "signs." If Jules had continued his criminal behavior, he would have deserved whatever misfortune that would have then followed. This is his one chance for salvation. Don't forget, as we are watching the ending of the movie, because of its non-linear chronology, we have already seen Vince (Jules's partner) getting killed by Butch the boxer, in another chance incident. This information (that only the audience knows) leads the audience to "agree" that Jules should heed the sign and leave the life of crime.

Pulp Fiction is not a classical take on destiny but connects story incidents of chance, necessity, and probability in a way that enhances the story's ACTION-IDEA, as well as its unique hipster soul. The fluctuation between chance elements and fate allows viewers to make up their own minds about destiny. This is why the movie is much more than a "cool flick" about two hoods spouting jive. Its structure makes it a masterpiece, and earned Quentin Tarantino an Oscar for best screenplay.

Evoking destiny by using the tools of chance, destiny, necessity, and probability to form ONE COMPLETE ACTION is a provocative way to shape screenplays. Shape yours this way, and someday you may be strutting down the aisle to accept an Oscar for your screenplay. And that would be no accident.

11.

Keep It in the Family . . .
The Tragic Deed

I once watched a CNN reporter ask a military old-timer to define what the "center of gravity" for winning a war was. He couldn't answer the reporter, but I fell in love with the concept of "center of gravity" as an analogy for an important aspect of what Aristotle teaches us about dramatic story and screenwriting. The center of gravity in dramatic story is simple: It's called the tragic deed. The tragic deed is the most intense, horrible thing that happens in the story. It usually is caused by the hero, or happens to the hero, and it involves:

> an action of a destructive or painful nature, such as murders, tortures, woundings, and the like.

It's a good idea to state the tragic deed in the ACTION-IDEA so you can keep the center of gravity of your story in mind. For an example of this, let's take a look at an ACTION-IDEA of another classic:

 **ROSEMARY'S BABY**—ROSEMARY'S husband makes a deal with SATAN WORSHIPPERS to have her raped by the devil and breed his child, so that he

can advance as an actor. Afterward, ROSEMARY tries to
discover why her pregnancy is difficult, and what her weird
neighbors want from her fetus, until she gives birth to the
devil's child and decides to mother it.

In *Rosemary's Baby*, Rosemary's husband (Guy), after
slipping her sleeping pills, delivers her to the devil worship-
pers and offers her body to Satan, who impregnates her. No
two ways about it, the devil having sex with Rosemary is
the tragic deed. Aristotle emphasizes an important aspect of
what makes it so horrific:

> In a deed of this description the parties must nec-
> essarily be either friends, or enemies, or indifferent to
> one another. Now when enemy does it on enemy, there
> is nothing to move us to pity either in his doing or in
> his meditating the deed, except so far as the actual pain
> of the sufferer is concerned; and the same is true when
> the parties are indifferent to one another. Whenever the
> tragic deed, however, is done within the family—when
> murder or the like is done or meditated by brother on
> brother, by son on father, by mother on son, or son on
> mother—these are the situations the poet should seek
> after.

That Rosemary's misery is caused by her own husband
greatly adds to the pity and horror we feel for her. If a sleazy
porno director tricked her, the scene would be scary, but it

wouldn't have the same magnitude. The tragic deed always involves the hero and something being done to the hero. It gives the story weight, a gravity to hold it down and keep all the other story elements floating around it like little satellites.

Theoretically, the tragic deed can happen anywhere in the story. It can even happen in the back story, before the actual movie begins, as in *Oedipus Rex*. Oedipus had met his father on the road and killed him, without knowing it was his father. This deed weighs the entire story down and ultimately connects to Oedipus blinding himself at the end of the play. The physical pain Oedipus feels when he gouges his eyes out matches his psychic pain. As Aristotle teaches us, the tragic deed usually involves the hero experiencing very intense physical suffering because of it. In *The Godfather*, the tragic deed is that Michael must kill members of his family because they are traitors. In *Titanic*, the tragic deed is Jack freezing in the icy Atlantic waters as he props up the wood raft to save Rose. (Aristotle implies that if the tragic deed doesn't actually happen to the hero then it should happen to a family relation or to someone *like* family, as Jack is to Rose in *Titanic*.)

Keep the tragic deed in the family, and use it as a strong center of gravity to give your screenplay rich, dramatic depth. It can happen in the beginning, as in *Rosemary's Baby*, or at the end, as it does in *Titanic*. Just make sure it happens.

12.

Oops! I Caused My Own Undeserved Misfortune Again

An imitation not only of a complete action, but also of incidents arousing pity and fear . . . pity is occasioned by undeserved misfortune, and fear by that of one like ourselves . . . the change in the hero's fortunes . . . must lie not in any depravity, but in some great error on his part.

The *Poetics* is so useful to screenwriters because Aristotle explains *why* we humans respond to dramatic story. Basically, we respond to dramatic story when we can relate to it. We need to feel that the misfortune the hero suffers is like our own, especially if it's going to arouse our pity and fear. We must pity the hero's misfortune and feel deeply about it, because that misfortune is undeserved, and we must fear it could happen to us. Pity and fear are a part of the deep emotional empathy we feel in watching a good dramatic story, be it *Rocky*, *The Godfather*, or *American Beauty*.

But how do we relate to movie heroes when we don't fight in gladiator arenas, consort with the devil, or battle the

Evil Empire of the Death Star? The answer is that like heroes in drama, we make choices that cause our own misfortune. We realize (after years of therapy) that we can't blame anyone else for our fate because we ourselves have caused it! No one was standing on the sidelines telling us what choices to make. So because bad stuff happens to us as a result of our own errors in judgment, we often feel that our own misfortune is "undeserved."

Take a quick hypothetical example: Jane tries to be an actress, risks her whole life on this dream, and at fifty-seven hasn't made it and has nothing. She has caused her misfortune; she made a choice, an error in judgment, and kept pursuing acting. But she doesn't really deserve such misfortune either, because at the time she made her decision to be an actress, she didn't know that she didn't have a chance to make it. Although she persists in pursuing her dream against all odds, we still feel that she doesn't deserve her misfortune and misery.

When misfortune that befalls a hero is both undeserved and caused by the hero, it arouses "pity" and "fear" in the audience. The hero must use reasoning (wrong reasoning), because drama works by illuminating the plight of conscious humankind. Despite the gift of creation that is our higher mind, we humans *still* screw up our lives. Aristotle points out that in drama, the causes of misfortune can't be depravity, because then the misfortune would be a result of our animal nature and therefore not interesting. You can call such bad judgment a "tragic flaw" if you like, but make sure you understand that Aristotle is clear on this concept: It is poor reasoning, not primal urges, that causes the hero's misfortune.

The beauty of an error in judgment is that you can use it to impact every single beat of the story, or just one time to set the plot up. In *Gladiator*, Maximus's error or "tragic flaw" is his pride, displayed when he refuses to honor Commodus, who has just stolen the throne. And that's it! This error in judgment sets off all the events that lead to his misfortune: Commodus has Maximus's wife and son killed, and Maximus is sent off to be executed; he escapes wounded, then becomes a slave, a gladiator, and although he restores the government to the people, he still dies. His pride, for which you can't blame him, causes his downfall. Now in Maximus's case, it's a pretty simple mistake. It happens once, and that's all the story needs. But this error in judgment adds a rich, tragic tone to *all* the misfortune that befalls him, precisely because he has actively caused his own fate.

Dramatic stories with happy endings use action based on the undeserved misfortunes of the hero as well. The obvious difference is that in happy dramatic stories, the hero overcomes the misfortune, as in *Rocky*. Rocky chooses to be a thumb breaker instead of a serious boxer, but that's soon fixed by Apollo, Mickey, and the Rock himself, who is determined to overcome his loser status in life.

Now let's turn our attention to actual misfortunes and draw on an analogy from life once again. What makes an undeserved misfortune weighty enough to carry a plot? If you park your new Rolls Royce in a run-down neighborhood overnight and come back to find your window smashed and radio stolen, is this an action on which you can build a story? It's a misfortune, it's (somewhat) undeserved, and it's caused by an error in judgment. However, an ACTION-IDEA that will arouse pity and fear in an audience must be based on undeserved misfortunes of *great magnitude*—on serious life-changing events that make you feel glad it isn't you. (And because it's caused by the hero's error in judgment, it could very well be you!) Here is a list of undeserved misfortunes that Aristotle, elsewhere in his writings, outlines as subject matters that arouse pity and fear in audiences:*

1. Death
2. Bodily assault or ill treatment
3. Old age, illness
4. Lack of food
5. Lack of friends
6. Ugliness
7. Weakness
8. Being crippled
9. Having your good expectations disappointed

---

*The following list is drawn from *The Therapy of Desire* by Martha Craven Nussbaum (Princeton, N.J.: Princeton University Press, 1996), p. 87, which cites the misfortunes that cause pity, as given in Aristotle's *Nicomachean Ethics*.

10. Having good things come too late
11. Having no good things happen to you
12. Having good things happen but being unable to enjoy them

Undeserved misfortunes destroy heroes like Maximus in *Gladiator*, or the hero overcomes them, as in *Rocky*. The key is, you don't just focus the whole story on one big undeserved event, you build all the significant scenes around the hero's major misfortune.

To do this, you can use a series of misfortunes, ones from the twelve itemized above, in individual scenes. Let's see how undeserved misfortunes work in *Gladiator*, starting with its ACTION-IDEA:

GLADIATOR—MAXIMUS, a brilliant Roman general, refuses to honor COMMODUS, and is sentenced to die. He escapes execution, and becomes a slave, a star gladiator, and returns to Rome to avenge the murder of his family by COMMODUS. He kills him in the arena after being mortally wounded in the back by him, restoring Rome to the senate as he dies.

There are several undeserved misfortunes just in the ACTION-IDEA: Maximus's family was murdered, he becomes a slave, and being a star gladiator wasn't a fate to be desired. But again, this chain of events is set in motion by

his error in judgment, occurring when he refused to acknowledge Commodus as Caesar, for which we can't blame
him and so we pity him when all these bad things happen
to him. Plus, because Maximus cares about his family and
refuses the advances of Lucilla, he seems honorable to us,
and his humanity makes him someone we relate to. In other
words, he seems like us, in our most tragic-heroic image of
ourselves, so we fear his bad fate can be ours as well.

The numerous misfortunes that befall Maximus serve
not only to propel the plot of *Gladiator* but to connect its
scenes thematically. For example, Maximus kills the barbarians (death) and wishes to return home but can't (having
good things happen but being unable to enjoy them). He
refuses to honor Commodus and is sentenced to die (death),
but he escapes and is wounded (bodily harm). He then is
captured as a slave and trained as a gladiator, where he must
defend himself against further bodily harm and death. He
fights other gladiators, who also don't deserve their misfortune, and has to kill them (death). Finally at the end, Commodus wounds him (bodily harm) and then he dies,
returning to heaven to join his wife and child.

Notice that in *Gladiator*, all the scenes are *organic* and
that they make sense in relation to the movie as a whole.
They are of similar tone and style and blend together well,
and they create ONE COMPLETE ACTION.

Even though the ending of *Gladiator* isn't really tragic
because Maximus goes to heaven when he dies, the movie
itself is still a classic tragedy. Maximus lives up to the mantra

of "strength and honor" that he utters in the opening scene as a general for Caesar. Because he suffers so much during the story, his life becomes a tragic demonstration of this very mantra.

The mistake in a hero's reasoning, leading to the hero's subsequent related misfortunes, is a great tool in building story action and in conveying profound truth to the audience. But remember: Aristotelian principles are not rules, they are starting points to understand how and why audiences respond to drama. Examining these principles and how they work will hopefully give you a handle on how to apply them to your own screenwriting.

May strength, honor, and peace be with you and your future audience!

13.

How a Little Moralizing Turned a Gladiator Gore Fest into a Best Picture

Tragedy is essentially an imitation not of persons but of action and life.

In the movie *Gladiator*, General Maximus tells his troops to "unleash hell" upon the barbarians immediately before his army's bloody clash with them. This sequence proceeds like any gratuitous battle scene should—blood splashing, limbs flying, swords clanging. Then the action on the screen turns into slow motion, the battle sounds dim, and the doleful musical score cranks up. The music is sad rather than thrilling because the movie is commenting on the fact that slaughtering these men raises what I call a moral contradiction: It is both right for Maximus to kill the barbarians, and wrong at the same time because it's just that—killing.

That is how a moral contradiction works in a dramatic story; the hero is right to take an action, and at the same time there is something morally wrong with that action. This is a secret ingredient to dramatic story that the *Poetics* teaches us to use, enabling the audience to see life imitated through the life of a hero, who is morally compromised in some way. Because *Gladiator* used this technique so effectively, it won Best Picture at the 2001 Academy Awards, despite being very gory—a decidedly unusual vote by the academy.

In *Gladiator*, there is no doubt that Maximus and his army are right in attacking the barbarians. Not only do we hear Caesar say that they are savages, but we watch the Germanians hold up the messenger's severed head and later send back his headless corpse as a response to Caesar's request for a peaceful surrender. But bloodshed is still bloodshed, and the tragic battle plays as a dark comment on the way human beings get things done. To paraphrase Caesar, the barbarians will have civilization brought to them. Ironically, the "civilized" ends of the Roman Empire must justify their brutal means.

Aristotle knew that his audiences were interested in moral questions, and when he told his students that tragedy is an "imitation of action and life," they automatically assumed he was referring to the moral life of a hero. When Maximus washes blood off his hands after the battle and stares into the bloodied water, the audience feels his anguish for having to kill the barbarians even though they are ruthless savages. His moral turmoil helps the audience relate to him even though it might not relate to the specific situation that he is in (i.e., slave-turned-gladiator).

All the action that brings change in the story must raise the central moral question. What brings change in *Gladiator* is fighting and killing. Albeit those of a brilliant general,

Maximus's actions, as we have seen, are inherently "right" and "wrong" at the same time. That the gladiators he must slaughter in self-defense aren't all enemies but have been victimized like himself, raises the same agonizing moral contradiction. All this "moralizing" helps us relate to the movie.

In our day-to-day efforts to survive, we all feel like the real world is a jungle. In showing a human tendency toward violence and revealing this as a tragic aspect of human nature, *Gladiator* imitates life and makes a statement about the human condition modern viewers can appreciate.

The message to you as a screenwriter is this: Don't shy away from using moral contradiction to spice up your screenplay stories. The audience *wants* to see right and wrong addressed, because everyone feels that this gets at the heart of what it is to be human. And just be glad that you're not getting up in the morning and strapping on gladiator gear for another day in the arena. Be glad that your own moral contradiction probably consists in competing with an associate for a promotion. Be glad—yes!—that after putting on the screenwriting armor of the *Poetics,* you can race out into the brutal arena of Hollywood and shout, "Bring 'em on!"

14.

A Movie Is Long Enough So
It Ends . . . Happy or Sad

As a rough general formula, [a tragedy should be] a length which allows of the hero passing by a series of probable or necessary stages from misfortune to happiness, or from happiness to misfortune . . .

This chapter will serve as an introduction to the very important dramatic concept of "reversal of fortune" and will be the subject of the next several chapters. Let's begin with a very rudimentary discussion of fortune itself. Fortune is that which determines whether a character ends up happy or sad and is the end result of the story's main action. In other words, Rocky lasts fifteen rounds, and this conclusion to *Rocky*'s ACTION-IDEA means that Rocky's story ends on a happy note.

Someone asked Abraham Lincoln, "How tall should a man be?" His response: "Tall enough until his feet reach the ground." This response is also similar to what Aristotle really means in the above excerpt, concerning how long a plot must be. The length of the story depends on whatever it requires for the movement from happiness or sadness to its opposite to take place. The individual scenes must be composed so that the change in fortune seems logical and satisfying to the audience.

Most great movies depict an extreme transformation of fortune. In fact, Aristotle's favorite kind of plot uses a device called "reversal of fortune," which means something happens to the hero that causes his fortune to reverse instantaneously.

As Aristotle points out, happiness is what every human being wants, and it follows that the hero's pursuit of happiness is of keen interest to an audience. The pursuit of happiness is so important that Aristotle describes it as our moral obligation. The ancient Greeks believed that it was every human being's moral obligation to pursue his or her own happiness, first and foremost, but to do so ethically. This is virtue.

Happiness in a story can mean remaining alive, and going to heaven, as Rose does in *Titanic*. The kids in *The Blair Witch Project* fail to stay alive, which results in a sad ending. Every scene must organically and logically lead up to the happy or sad conclusion of a movie: A scene is virtually a mini-story, structured like a mini-action idea. For example, the scene where Rocky first jogs up the steps as part of his training and can't make it ends on a sad note. The scene where Rocky tries to help the tramp girl get off the streets while she curses him out is a scene with a sad ending. The scene where Rocky finally jogs up the steps and is able to make it to the top is a scene with a happy ending. Aristotle goes so far as to say that the fortune of the hero develops in logical stages.

In *Rocky*, Aristotle's "formula" works in a pretty straightforward fashion. Even Rocky's reversal of fortune is textbook. Rocky starts off badly and *then* gets a shot at the crown. He's a total bum-loser; he's not even a good loan shark and gets his brains beaten in for sixty dollars a night in a basement. To go from that state of affairs to lasting fifteen rounds against the champ is an extreme reversal of fortune. But how Rocky gets there is through logical stages in the form of scenes or "mini-stories" that have happy and sad conclusions. *Rocky*'s "mini-stories" add up to the sum total of Rocky's transformation, so to speak.

As an audience, we can only know if movies and scenes end happily or sadly by the actions the characters take:

> Tragedy is essentially an imitation not of persons but of action and life, of happiness and misery. All human happiness or misery takes the form of action: the end aimed at is a certain kind of activity, not a quality . . . It is in our actions—*what we do*—that we are happy or the reverse.

All the audience needs to interpret whether a scene or movie has ended happily or sadly can be dialog, or simply a gesture from a character in a reaction shot, but the kind of action that usually works best to communicate emotional conclusions is physical and demonstrative. For example, when Rocky finally rises during the fifteenth round of the boxing match right before the referee counts him out, this shows that he lasted fifteen rounds, and this action means Rocky is happy. And this moment is not just a change in Rocky's fortune, it's a *reversal* of fortune—it carries the weight and emotions of the whole plot.

You may be interested to find out that practically every great movie depicts an extreme change in the hero's fortune. It's as if we moviegoers were fortune-change junkies. So don't underestimate the severity of this need in the audience. The hero's fortune must go from one extreme to the other, and how it gets where it's going must be presented *logically*, and entertainingly. Another little secret about this I've noticed is that many great screenwriters have figured out how to have it all still come down to one moment as well, as we noted earlier in *Rocky*. With that thought in mind, it's time to take a look at how the concept of reversal of fortune works in the context of Aristotle's favorite kind of plot. On to the next chapter!

15.

If You're Happy and You Know It . . . Time for a Reversal of Fortune and Discovery

The most powerful elements of attraction in Tragedy, the [reversal of fortune] and Discoveries, are parts of the Plot.

This and the next few chapters will zero in on Aristotle's favorite kind of plot, one that includes a reversal of fortune combined with a discovery, which he called a "complex plot." Not only does the hero's fortune undergo extreme reversal but a movement from extreme ignorance to profound knowledge (the "discovery") takes place. For the complex plot to do its job (take the audience to the height of pity and fear), Aristotle insists that the reversal of fortune/ discovery be *caused* by the main action:

[Reversal of fortune and discovery] should each of them arise out of the structure of the Plot itself [the main action], so as to be the *consequence, necessary or probable, of the antecedents.*

American Beauty follows this principle closely while fashioning a complex plot with an original spin. The plot centers on Lester's infatuation with sixteen-year-old Angela and the actions he takes as a result. However, while this main action definitely leads to Lester's murder (reversal of fortune), it does so in an indirect way. Colonel Fitz, who finally murders Lester, is not connected with Lester's pursuit of Angela but is turned on by Lester when he notices Lester lifting weights in his quest to look and feel younger. Lester rejects the Colonel's advances, and then ends up almost having sex with Angela, but decides against it when he learns that she's a virgin. Lester's *discovery* occurs when he's learned that Angela is a virgin, which brings him back to reality and causes him to see her for who she is—a confused teenage girl. A reversal from complete ignorance (he thought she was promiscuous) to complete knowledge (she's an innocent virgin) takes place. Choosing not to seduce a sixteen-year-old when given the chance, Lester recaptures his dignity. His happiness peaks in this recognition of his own self-worth, but then Colonel Fitz shoots him. The two moments effect a complete reversal, from extremely good fortune (I do have integrity) to extremely bad fortune (I'm dead). By having the hero cause his own reversal of fortune (death), but indirectly, *American Beauty* realizes a complex plot with a unique twist. And this structure of *American Beauty* made it have a tremendous impact on its audience.

There's a reason the complex plot has stayed around so long: It works! Find new ways of using it the way the Oscar-winning screenplay for *American Beauty* did. Or at least learn from it to understand how and why plot structures impact audiences the way they do. If you do decide to reinvent a way to use reversal of fortune/discovery, remember, it's Aristotle's favorite plot device. By using it in any fashion, you can't go wrong.

16.

"It Scared Me Because I Saw It Coming" . . . The Rolls Royce of Complex Plots

The best of all Discoveries, however, is . . . when the great surprise comes about through a probable incident.

For Aristotle, what we would call the Rolls Royce of complex plots is one in which the discovery is a "big surprise." And not just a big surprise, a probable or even *predictable* surprise! This is possible because the story plants little hints for the audience, but not enough to give the surprise away. It's kind of like knowing someone is planning a surprise party for you; there are clues but you're never 100 percent sure.

For example, in *Rosemary's Baby*, Rosemary wanders into Minnie's apartment and gets to see the little bundle of evil she has just given birth to. At this moment a reversal of fortune occurs—Rosemary realizes that her child has lived (she thought it had died)—and the big surprise is that it's the spawn of Satan. Rosemary gasps when she recognizes in her baby the red eyes she'd glimpsed the night the devil himself impregnated her. But that night ("baby night," as her husband refers to it), she was half-asleep and unsure of what had happened. Now she *is* sure, and instantly every puzzling story incident that has led up to this point makes sense to her and to the audience. The surprise is a predictable one, but we can still experience intense pity and fear for Rosemary.

Where do I get off calling the chilling ending to *Rosemary's Baby* a "surprise," when we knew what was going to happen all along? We knew it when we saw Rosemary wake up during "baby night" and glimpse the devil impregnating her. We knew why Minnie fed her those disgusting cakes and why her husband got scared when he felt the baby kick in her stomach. And we knew that the intense pain she felt inside her pregnant belly wasn't indigestion. At the end of the movie, we're still surprised. Why?

I'll tell you why. That's what we pay for. We have a dual brain when we watch a movie; part of us participates in it, identifying with poor Rosemary and her situation, and part of us stands outside of it all as a spectator who can see what's going on. We have to watch, but we want to participate, no matter how emotionally wrenching our movie experience. As incredible as it may seem, we allow the filmmakers to play with our heads. I've seen *Rosemary's Baby* a million times, and I'm *still* surprised, like Rosemary herself, when she beholds her baby Lucifer.

The key is in the balance between what we are shown and what we aren't shown. What if instead of just *suggesting* that the devil impregnates Rosemary, the movie showed us everything. Imagine the devil flying out from hell, flapping his wings around the room, and then proceeding to mock Christianity and rape Rosemary, all of course using computer graphics. There would be no ambiguity as to what happened to Rosemary, no keeping the audience off balance, no big surprise waiting to happen, no pity and fear, and no enduring classic. It would be a special-effects Hollywood bomb deriving its juice from spectacle, a tendency of weak dramas that Aristotle warned us to avoid, so long ago.

When the discovery portion of a complex plot comes as predictable surprise, it truly is the Rolls Royce of complex plots. It's a first-class vehicle to take an audience to the height of pity and fear, which delivers the best catharsis.

17.

The Devil Is in the Realistic Details of the Plot of *Angel Heart*

... artifice must be reserved for matters outside the play—for past events beyond human knowledge, or events yet to come, which require to be foretold or announced; since it is the privilege of the Gods to know everything. [Therefore] there should be nothing improbable among the actual incidents. If it be unavoidable, however, [improbable incidents] should be outside the tragedy ...

This chapter looks at reversal of fortune/discovery, or "complex plot," from yet another angle. This time we're going to see how when a powerful fantasy/horror back story is revealed through a realistic complex plot, it can have an explosive impact on the audience.

Aristotle tells us that in the dramatic plots, "improbable deeds" should be kept in back story (before the play), because drama needs to be realistic to work. All "artifice" or things outside of known reality, including the power of gods and devils, must occur outside of what we see on screen. The simple reason is, drama works best if it only shows a level of reality that is recognizable. Even modern horror movies can use a realistic plot structure to make their fantasy horror realms seem strikingly realistic.

Take *Angel Heart*. In this movie, we never see the story's powerful fantasy/horror deeds take place, because the movie restricts them to the back story. However, it cleverly uses realistic plot action during the movie to *reveal* the power and reality of these deeds. By showing Harry Angel carrying out realistic murders during the plot, this proves that he also committed horrible deeds in the back story. *Angel Heart* avoids spectacle, using structure effectively to create its fantasy/horror realm:

> The tragic fear and pity may be aroused by the Spectacle; but they may also be aroused by the very structure and incidents of the play—which is the better way and shows the better poet.

Before the movie *Angel Heart* even begins, Johnny Favorite, a powerful devil worshipper, has conjured up the devil and sold his soul to him so he could become a famous crooner. Later, Johnny discovers an ancient rite whereby he can steal the soul of a man and use it to hide out from the devil. Johnny, Toots Sweets, and his girlfriend Margaret Krusemark bring unsuspecting Harry Angel back to a hotel, where Johnny slices Harry's heart out and eats it as they chant incantations. It works: Johnny steals Harry's soul and becomes invisible to the devil. He even looks like Harry and eventually, because he suffers amnesia from serving in World War II, he thinks he *is* Harry. But this is all back story.

After the movie begins, the plot uses scenes of recognizable reality, including those in the beginning, when the devil (disguised as "Louis Cyphre") hires "Harry" to find Johnny. Harry, now a private detective, investigates people who knew Johnny, like Toots and Margaret. One by one, the people Harry interviews turn up dead. The story plays more like a realistic detective movie than a horror flick. Harry becomes increasingly more nervous because he believes someone is trying to frame him for the murders. The audience hasn't seen the murders take place, but Harry discovers the dead bodies of the people he interviews after he leaves them and returns. Eventually, Margaret's father Ethan fills Harry in, telling him about his horrific past deeds, causing him to remember he is Johnny Favorite. This incorporation of the back story into the plot demonstrates the essence of great plotting: causally related action that brings change to the hero, moving the hero toward a reversal of fortune.

After Harry discovers who he really is, he runs back to Margaret (already murdered) and finds the dog tags she kept from the victim that Johnny killed. Harry reads his own name on them, "Harry Angel." This begins the *denouement*: The devil appears and plays Harry a "Johnny Favorite" recording, which helps Harry recall that it was he who murdered all the people he interviewed. The movie cuts to Harry's POV (point of view) as he now finally recalls in flashbacks killing the four people, unconsciously guided by the devil. This twenty-second montage is as great an "unraveling" as any denouement can contain. It avoids being overly explicit (relying on spectacle) and becomes in effect a *tragic deed* because the people he murdered were like family to him. The brief images of Harry killing the four people are used to jar his memory (recognition entailing *discovery*) that he's searching for himself and is the evil Johnny Favorite. Thereupon he undergoes a *reversal of fortune* (I'm going to hell).

Angel Heart's complex plot structure works because the fantastical horror elements that are kept in the back story connect to the murders that Harry commits during the action that plays out on the screen. The plot also works because it plays on the audience's psyche:

> . . . incidents have the very greatest effect on the mind when they occur unexpectedly and at the same time in consequence of one another.

We unconsciously sense Harry is murdering the people when he leaves them, which arouses our deepest, innermost fears, yet we also don't want to discover he is the murderer because we like him. *Angel Heart* works its magic on us every step of the way by using structure instead of spectacle.

One final note in conclusion: Never sign a contract with anyone by the name of Louis Cyphre, because God only knows what he'll make you do. Use the God-like wisdom of the *Poetics* to write a great script and get your break into the movie business.

18.

Whatever Causes the Action Better Be Up There on the Screen

The tragic pleasure is that of pity and fear, and the poet has to produce it by a work of imitation; it is clear, therefore, that the causes [of the action that can arouse pity and fear] should be included in the incidents of his story.

Aristotle tells us that the "causes" of the action that arouse the audience's pity and fear must be included in the story. What does he mean? In a nutshell, he's telling us that it is not enough for the audience to be "told" that a hero's fortune has reversed. The audience must *experience* a systematic buildup through "stages," culminating in the hero's reversal of fortune in a way that arouses their empathy.

For example, take a look at *Citizen Kane*. The causes of the action that arouses our pity and fear are simple, starting with the first cause of action: Young Charles Kane is taken from his home because of an inheritance that prompts his mother to send him away with Mr. Thatcher, a guardian his mother has hired to raise her son. Charles's undeserved misfortune affects his entire life; he becomes controlling and selfish as an adult and dies an old, lonely man. Because we understand *why* he got that way, the plot arouses our pity and fear. For Aristotle, all this is revealed by a very special definition of character:

> There are in the natural order of things, therefore, two causes—Character and Thought—of their actions, and consequently of their success or failure in their lives.

To Aristotle, "character" refers strictly to the moral quality of a person *revealed* through his or her thoughts and the actions stemming from these thoughts. For example, if you plot to rob a bank, you must first "think" about taking such an action before performing it. But it's the *thought* behind this action that reveals your "character," isn't it? In other words, if you are robbing a bank to pay for your girlfriend's diamond necklace, you're a "bad person." But if you're robbing a bank to feed the homeless people, that reveals a different "character." It's the same in movies: The "thought" that leads to the key actions reveals the "character" of the hero in the story and must be of a nature that arouses the audience's pity and fear.

Let's return to *Angel Heart*: Harry hears Ethan tell the back story of how Johnny ate a man's heart to steal his soul. Harry's "thought" or remembrance of this deed causes Harry to vomit, telling us that he is morally repulsed, and thus his moral character is *revealed*. This cause of action leads Harry closer to his eternal reversal of fortune (going to hell). But the fact that Harry realizes the moral implications of his actions help us feel for him. We have seen that he truly regrets his behavior and have known him to be a moral character, so we relate to him.

To close, I'd like to sum up this chapter thus:

A plot must include causes of the action that can arouse the audience's deepest pity and fear. This means the audience must understand the hero's thoughts and see those thoughts becoming actions, which in turn reveal a moral quality (character) of the hero. This will help the audience to relate to the hero and feel empathy for him or her.

19.

A Movie Gave You a Bad Case of Pity and Fear? The Doctor Recommends a Catharsis

... With incidents arousing pity and fear, wherewith to accomplish its catharsis of such emotions.

In the final moments of a movie, the audience experiences the moment that allows them to purge themselves of pity and fear built up through the plot structure. Through this "catharsis," the audience releases not just the emotions the movie has stirred up in them, but they also dump other psychic garbage they've been carrying around. Catharsis leaves the audience with a renewed sense of mental clarity and better able to function in life. According to Aristotle, catharsis works best if *everything* in the story builds toward creating this one experience. The key is to understand that catharsis doesn't just "happen" in the final moments of a movie; it builds throughout the story up until the final *release*.

One of the most cathartic movies ever made is *Titanic*, if the scores of young girls who watched it at least ten times and wept each time is any indication. This isn't because of spectacle, although *Titanic* had spectacle in spades. It's because the movie is perfectly structured in terms of evoking a sense of young love and then taking the young lovers (Jack and Rose) on an adventure, during the course of which they not only bond but live through one of the most tragic events in history. Every emotion we feel grows out of their love story, which we experience as the plot develops, ever pulling at our heartstrings. And every moment of pity and fear builds to the moment of catharsis. The plot action is "supercharged" during the reversal of fortune/discovery scene when Jack freezes saving Rose.

Jack not only dies to save Rose, but suffers intensely in doing so. The combination of physical suffering and emotional suffering helps intensify the emotions of the audience, who, feeling the tragedy in their very bones, are swept away. This intense physical suffering allows the audience to experience a deeper catharsis when it comes.

It comes when the much older Rose finally lies down in her cabin bed and dies, joining Jack in heaven. *This* is where the audience releases their burden of pity and fear and finally experiences catharsis.

Titanic teaches us an important lesson in structure: Just as the plot must build to the reversal of fortune/discovery moment, so must catharsis. In other words, you must keep catharsis in mind as you structure the plot of your screen play. The entire plot of *Titanic* leading up to the scene where Jack dies and Rose is saved builds in a way that makes us really care about the couple and their relationship. Jack and Rose are in essence a "joint protagonist," inseparable in death as in life. Their fate affirms that it is in eternal love that the meaning of life resides—the story's theme.

Although Aristotle teaches us that catharsis is aided by all the spectacle the medium of drama has to offer, it's essentially structure that does the trick. Not that having Leo, Kate, a billion dollars, and a little Celine Dion hurt *Titanic*. It's just that, without great structure, *Titanic* the movie would have sunk faster than the real doomed ocean liner did.

20.

Action Speaks Louder Than Words, and Together They Can Speak Volumes!

Hence poetry is something more philosophic and of graver import than history, since its statements are of . . . universals . . . what such or such a kind of man will probably or necessarily say or do— which is the aim of poetry . . .

Someone once complained to a big studio boss in the golden years of Hollywood that movies weren't deep and he replied, "If you want to send a message, use Western Union."

How cynical can you get, you may be thinking. But perhaps the studio boss was saying more than meets the ears. Action, make that plot action, can be a very effective way to make universal statements about the human condition.

When dialog complements action, a screenplay can speak volumes. Your movie will be even more "philosophical than history," to paraphrase Aristotle. Indeed, the kernel of truth the screenwriter is seeking to convey must be clearly articulated early in the writing process:

. . . simplify and reduce [your story] to a universal
form, before proceeding to lengthen it out by the inser-
tion of episodes.

Which brings us back to our humble tool, the ACTION-
IDEA. Let's re-examine the ACTION-IDEA of *American
Beauty*, which I've broken down here into three parts for
easier reference:

AMERICAN BEAUTY—(1) LESTER, a
middle-aged man, whose wife and daughter think
he's a loser, has lost all desire for life. (2) LESTER gets infatuated with sixteen-year-old ANGELA, causing him to get
fired, smoke pot, and work out. He catches the eye of his
neighbor COLONEL FITZ, a Neo-Nazi homophobe. (3) After
rejecting a sexual advance from the COLONEL, LESTER almost has sex with ANGELA, but learns she's a virgin and
decides not to have sex with her, thereby regaining his dignity. Then COLONEL FITZ murders him, and in his dying
moments Lester realizes the beauty of just being alive.

Compare this to the universal message of the movie:

Appreciate the simple beauty of life and enjoy it while you
have it.

All the action is geared to the expression of the message. In
part 1, Lester as the unhappy middle-aged man is a great

initial "universal" setup that will interest an audience, who should have no problem relating to Lester's condition. It also is easy to see how, in part 2, he falls for Angela and begins to lead a marginal but more satisfying existence while inadvertently generating the course of events culminating in his death in part 3. It's as though part 1 and part 2 act in opposition to each other to produce a result, part 3 (per Aristotle's technique of dialectic, incidentally, which we'll get to later).

As we saw in chapter 4 and as demonstrated here schematically, all of the action, and all of its basic components (the "parts" of the ACTION-IDEA) work together to form ONE COMPLETE ACTION, which delivers unequivocally the message of the film. This message (to reiterate), "appreciate the simple beauty of life and enjoy it while you have it," has been stated both by the structure of the action and by Lester's narration at the end. The structure and dialog deliver a powerful movie message, more powerful and immediate than by sending it Western Union.

21.

The Perfect Hollywood Sad/ Happy Plot versus the Perfect *Poetics* Sad Plot

*[In a perfect Plot] the change in the hero's for-
tunes must be not from misery to happiness, but on
the contrary from happiness to misery; and the
cause of it must lie not in any depravity, but in
some great error on his part; the man himself being
either such as we have described, or better, not
worse, than that. Fact also confirms our theory.*

For tragedy to really work, Aristotle demands that a hero's fortune move from happiness to misery. This is his *dream* plot, but he stated earlier that tragic plots *could* move in the reverse direction and end happily. As I said earlier, "tragedy" (as used in the *Poetics*) indicates "serious drama that is realistic." It doesn't necessarily mean down-beat. In Aristotle's day, audiences responded best to dark tragedies like *Oedipus* or *Antigone*, so he formulated a perfect-plot theory in accordance with this observation.

But that was ancient Greece. This is now. Tales of un-remitting gloom, however cathartic, do not appeal to the general public anymore. People desire emotional release, but they also crave escape. So how have modern screenwriters managed to adapt the Aristotelian "perfect plot" to suit modern tastes?

Many popular movies use a Hollywood story technique I've come to call the "happy/sad ending," whereby dramas of tragic stature succeed despite ending on an upbeat note.

Gladiator is also an example of how a modern-day movie actually twists Aristotle's concept into a whole new kind of "perfect plot." Maximus starts off as happy, good, and honorable. His wife and son are murdered; he then becomes a slave and gladiator and is finally killed by Commodus, the evil Caesar. However, Maximus does not wind up miserable, because he dies and joins his family in heaven. This isn't just implied—we see his wife and son smiling as he is reunited with them after he dies and his spirit leaves his body. Maximus doesn't simply move from happiness to misery. The "going to heaven" trick gives *Gladiator* a happy/sad ending.

For a more complete understanding of what Aristotle meant by the perfect plot, let's see what he has to say about three kinds of plots he guards against:

> . . . there are three forms of Plot to be avoided:
>
> (1) A good man must not be seen passing from happiness to misery, or
>
> (2) a bad man [must not be seen passing] from misery to happiness. The first situation is not fear-inspiring or piteous, but simply odious to us. This second is

the most untragic that can be; it has no one of the
requisites of Tragedy; it does not appeal either to the
human feeling in us, or to our pity, or to our fears.

(3) Nor, on the other hand should an extremely bad man
be seen falling from happiness into misery. Such a
story may arouse the human feeling in us, but it will
not move us to either pity or fear; pity is occasioned
by undeserved misfortune, and fear by that of one
like ourselves; so that there will be nothing either
piteous or fear-inspiring in this situation.

Notice that whether a hero is "good" or "bad" is just as
important as which direction the reversal of fortune takes,
and we must relate to a hero in order to be moved by the
plot—the hero must be "like us." As we will discuss further,
in the following chapter, the best (tragic/dramatic) plot has
a hero who is a mixture of good and bad qualities, leaning
toward goodness (like us) and whose life goes from good
fortune to bad fortune.

For an updated version of Greek tragedy, let's look at
the plot of *Citizen Kane* (perfect by Aristotle's standards!).
The hero, Charles Foster Kane, is an average lower-middle-
class kid, who inherits a gigantic sum of money, and his
mother gives him away to a guardian, Mr. Thatcher. He
tries to make up for this lack of love by gaining money and
power, but in the process of doing so becomes a rigid and
uncaring scoundrel. However, since we the audience know
about Kane's childhood misfortunes, we see him as some-

where in between good and bad, because there are certainly things about his personality that we like. He tries to do good in his own way. He tries to use money to help the poor, even though it's for selfish reasons. He tries to use his newspaper for "good" political reasons, even though running through it all are his own special needs. But his fortune is undeserved, as we saw earlier in chapter 18, and obviously it moves from happiness to misery. What is unique in all this perfect plotting is that, in a typically American way, Kane's financial power and status were grafted onto him; he would have been happier leading a simple life with a loving family. Indeed *Citizen Kane* is a "perfect" American tragedy, just as *Oedipus Rex* is a "perfect" Greek one. No sad/happy ending needed, you notice, for what is considered by many to be the greatest movie of all time. The regular sad ending here did just fine.

22.

Move Your Audience by Teaching Them What They Already Know

. . . for if one has not seen the thing before, one's pleasure will not be in the picture as an imitation of it.

Aristotle believed dramatic story must present identifiable reality for the audience to be able to receive pleasure from it. Pity, fear, and catharsis come not from learning new esoteric facts but from a *re*-cognition of what one *already* thinks and feels. Scenes that are presented need not be based on the *particulars* of people's lives, but on *archetypical experience*. This is why it's important to build actions on "universals"—to substantiate universal truths about the human condition through the action of the plot.

It's a Wonderful Life entertains us while delivering a truth about the moral effect of human action upon others and oneself. It represents a reality that audiences understand easily so they can recognize themselves and be moved emotionally. The plot utilizes fantasy by having an angel (Clarence) show George Bailey how life would be worse without him, which brings about George's faith in himself.

Aristotle does not preach that a dramatic hero must necessarily have an altruistic self-sacrificing mission; sometimes the greatest effect a hero has is upon himself (as in *Rocky*). But in *It's a Wonderful Life*, Clarence the angel shows George how his actions have affected his family and neighbors by showing a *possible* world without him. The story's key emotional/cognitive peaks are identifiable as archetypical events (i.e., from *everyone's* life) that trigger emotional and mental clarity about the importance of our place and the effect of our actions on the world. In this way, the film moves us to a catharsis.

It's not just what Clarence shows George about the past that is archetypical ammunition for the audience to identify with. True to Aristotelian principles, the entire story action serves in this capacity as well. For example, the scene where George visits Mary at her house and is resentful because in his heart he knows she is his destiny, portrays a typical male response to the feeling of being pulled in by a girl who is going to settle him down to a more mundane life. It's also typical perhaps of the female point of view of having to "lasso in" the male. In fifties garb, the particulars of what George goes through represent basic human experiences. It's why we respond so profoundly to the story. In essence, it's our (perhaps not so wonderful at times) life.

The genius of *It's a Wonderful Life* is that it succeeds in telling us about life because it shows us our own life. Our pleasure is as an "imitation" of the picture: We've all been there and done that, and so it goes, *in perpetuum*. It's a wonderful life, and it will get even better when a studio executive recognizes himself or herself in your work and buys your screenplay.

23.

The Good, the Bad, and the Intermediate Hero

Character in a play is that which reveals the moral purpose of the agents . . . First and foremost . . . they shall be good.

In *Angel Heart*, we see the moral quality of Harry Angel revealed as his "thought" becomes action: Harry remembers the time he ate a man's heart and he throws up as he recalls this horrible deed he committed in the past. He's morally repulsed. That's his "character." Aristotle says that a hero must be "good," but Harry Angel murders four people in the plot, so he's anything *but* good. So how come *Angel Heart* works? It works because Harry doesn't know what he's doing when he kills the four people; his soul has been taken over by the evil Johnny Favorite. Even so, Harry manages to resist the devil in control of his mind and avoids killing his own daughter. Part of him is good and part of him is evil. This "split" between good and evil is precisely why *Angel Heart* works, as Aristotle points out:

There remains, then, the *intermediate* [between good and bad] kind of person, a man not pre-eminently virtuous and just, whose misfortune, however, is brought upon him not by vice and depravity but by some error of judgement.

When Aristotle says a hero must be good, he means that the hero must be *tending toward* goodness. It's this intermediate kind of hero that audiences relate to because they imagine themselves as both good *and* bad, or human. In *It's a Wonderful Life*, George Bailey is mostly good. He gives up his dreams of leaving Bedford Falls to help his local neighbors. But near the end of the story, when there is a crisis, George wants to abandon his family and neighbors and kill himself. In our eyes, George's utter despair makes him human, as do his struggles with life, which nearly break him.

In *Angel Heart* and *It's a Wonderful Life* the heroes have mixtures of good and bad in them, but it's the balance in each of the heroes that gives the stories their individual flavor and tone. According to Aristotle, this mixture of good and evil is what determines the characterization of not only the hero but all the personages in a dramatic story:

> The objects the imitator represents are actions, with agents who are necessarily either good men or bad—the diversities of human character being nearly always derivative from this primary distinction, since *the line between virtue and vice is one dividing the whole of mankind.* It follows, therefore, that the agents represented must be

either above our own level of goodness, or beneath it, or just such as we are . . .

In *Rocky*, there are people above Rocky's level of goodness and people who function below his level of goodness. Rocky is smack at "ground zero" of goodness, approaching superior goodness, which is why we like and relate to him. He proves this goodness trying to help Paulie, taking Mickey as a manager, dating Adrienne, saving the tramp girl, and so forth. In the end he completely transcends his loser status when he lasts fifteen rounds against Apollo Creed. But Adrienne's character falls above the "dividing line of virtue and vice," as Aristotle would put it," approaching sainthood, as we see through her devotion to Rocky despite her categorical opposition to boxing. Paulie and Mickey are just a hair below this dividing line (which is what you'd want in a boxing manager and trainer). Far down below the line is Apollo Creed, which makes the story work, because we are supposed to hate him. Apollo makes fun of Rocky's ethnic background, and when he comes out to fight he makes fun of America and acts like a buffoon. We sense that Apollo was also once a "bum from his neighborhood," who made it out but did not learn from his experience. He doesn't seem interested in helping his own neighbors transcend their status, as we know Rocky will.

In the ACTION-IDEA of your screenplay, the hero should reside, like Rocky, at the dividing line of goodness and badness, against which the other personages can be measured and around which their characters develop. This sort of moral orchestration will give your screenplay tone and depth, and lift it above the ordinary. Then the question won't be whether it's good, bad, or in between, but whether it's excellent, superb, or outstanding!

24.

It's the Thought Behind the Action That Counts: Creating the Tone of Your Screenplay

The action involves agents, who must necessarily have their distinctive qualities both of character and thought, since it is from these that we ascribe certain qualities to their actions.

Tone is a tough aspect of screenwriting and many writers blow it. Nothing, however, could be more crucial. We have seen how necessary unified action is to the dramatic impact of a story. The unified emotional quality or tone of the story action is no less essential. Aristotle gives us an important clue about how to achieve unity of tone, in pointing out the importance of the makeup of the "agents" of the action, whose "distinctive qualities of character and thought" make an impression on the audience and influence its perceptions. In other words, they set the tone.

The inner thoughts of a story's characters serve to reveal the motives for their actions and do so in such a way as to give a movie its characteristic flavor. In the teen movie *Can't Hardly Wait*, we quickly come to understand that the character of Mike is on the bad side of the "dividing line of goodness," because he dumps Amanda for the wrong reason: wanting to have sex with as many women as possible before leaving for college. Though he is unsuccessful in achieving this goal, he has been branded as the bad guy in our minds, because we're influenced when we learn his reasons for dumping his girlfriend. On the other hand, Preston (the hero) has harbored a crush on Amanda for years. It's his innocent belief that he and Amanda are meant to be together that makes the audience ascribe a positive quality to him and the actions he takes (e.g., giving her a love letter). The same goes for the other characters in the movie, such as Kenny and Denise, who, after getting locked in a bathroom, discover that they are not so different from each other. Through their thoughts we come to understand Kenny's childish, self-defensive actions and why Denise is so intolerant of him (he was mean to her in elementary school). In other words, we are allowed to look behind the personas of all the characters, whose actions assume humor and pathos as a result.

Thus we see how, within the framework of ONE COMPLETE ACTION, the moral attributes of the "agents" revealed through the reasoning behind their actions give your story its tone. In more simple terms: Pay attention to tone because it will enhance the quality of your screenplay. And remember: It's the thought behind the actions that count . . .

25

How to Cheat If You Can't Hire a Whole Chorus

The Chorus too should be regarded as one of the actors; it should be an integral part of the whole, and take a share in the action . . .

In Aristotle's day, staging a play involved using a chorus line of paid actors and singers that would stand in front of the stage, sing, and comment to the audience on the action. This helped develop the "magnitude" of the action without adding extraneous incidents to the ACTION-IDEA. For example, in *Oedipus Rex*, the chorus makes a statement after Oedipus is charged by his subjects to find the source of the plague in the city:

CHORUS (Citizens of Thebes):

Sweet is the voice of the god, that sounds in the Golden shrine of Delphi
What message has it sent to Thebes? My trembling Heart is torn with anguish.
Thou god of Healing, Phoebus Apollo
How do I fear! What has thou in mind

> *To bring upon us now? What is to be fulfilled*
> *From days of old?*
> *Tell me this, O Voice divine*
> *Thou child of Golden Hope*

The chorus here does not move the plot along but makes moral comments on what is happening by raising questions. This ancient technique is not used in modern drama, although modern versions of it can be found. For example, in *Something About Mary*, the two guys who sit in the trees and sing about the action are as close to a chorus in Greek theater as has ever existed in modern film. Notice how the "chorus" in this movie makes appearances, comments on the action, embellishes its meaning and emotional impact, while not really adding anything to the plot. Notice how this "chorus" keeps you at arm's length from the action while giving you a window into it. The viewer feels like a privileged spectator and at the same time becomes better connected to Ted the hero, who finally gets Mary. *Something About Mary* is an example of a comical way to use a chorus, serving the overall tone of the story.

Remember, the important thing in trying to use a modern chorus is to understand the chorus's job—to comment on the action and to reinforce it in the audience's perception. You can have all kinds of secondary characters commenting on the action. For a quick example of this, consider *The Terminator*, where Reese is held in the police station and questioned by a psychiatrist, who thinks he's crazy. The shrink and the cops are a perfect example of "chorus" commenting on the action. The questions and comments of the cops and the psychiatrist help to validate and explain the reality of the Terminator's mission, of Reese's role, and of Sarah's role in saving the future of the world.

In constructing the ACTION-IDEA of your screenplay, consider how using secondary characters as members of a "chorus" might work to strengthen it. If you're into far-fetched plots, a chorus may be key in making sure the audience understands what in the hell is going on.

26.

How to Create Characters That Are Really Really *Really* Alive

In the Characters there are four points to aim at. First and foremost, that they shall be good. There will be an element of character in the play, if (as has been observed) what a personage says or does reveals a certain moral purpose; and a good element of character, if the purpose so revealed is good . . . The second point is to make them appropriate . . . The third is to make them like the reality, which is not the same as their being good and appropriate, in our sense of the term. The fourth is to make them consistent and the same throughout . . .

One of the many things we can thank Aristotle for is his writings on how to create characters that seem both realistic *and* able to captivate an audience. First, make them good enough that we can root for them. Second, make them "appropriate," meaning give them characteristics that make sense for the type of person they are. Third, make them human—give them flaws or quirks that make us believe that they exist. Finally, whatever characteristics you do give them, make sure you keep them there throughout the length of the screenplay. As Aristotle says, make sure they are "consistently inconsistent."

In another passage, Aristotle elaborates on what he means by making a characer realistic. Once again, he uses painting as an analogy:

> As Tragedy is an imitation of persons better than the ordinary man, we in our way should follow the example of good portrait-painters, who reproduce the distinctive features of a man, and at the same time, without losing the likeness, make him handsomer than he is. The poet in like manner, in portraying men quick or slow to anger, or with similar infirmities of character, must know how to represent them as such, and at the same time as good men . . .

Rocky, trying in a larger-than-life way to be more than a bum from the neighborhood, is still oddly recognizable as a regular guy. Lester Burnham from *American Beauty* is the ultimate mid-life-crisis guy who eventually redeems himself in declining to sleep with Angela. Even Michael Corleone, the mafia son par excellence, appears noble in a time of family crisis because he is willing to defend and honor his family. In their actions and attributes, these three characters illustrate the realism to which tragic drama, according to Aristotle, should aspire. Additionally, he gives us five principles of life that we can use to create character in our stories:*

1. Nutritive Life
2. Desiring Life
3. Sensitive Life
4. Locomotion
5. Capacity for Rational Thought

Because these five principles all belong to the makeup of a real-life person's "psychology," they can be used to create convincing three-dimensional characters. Let's examine each one.

1. **Nutritive Life.** Do you wonder about your characters' eating habits? Wouldn't that tell you (and your audience) a lot about them? Don't your eating habits say a lot about you? You should brainstorm as much as you can to get a clear picture of what the eating habits of your characters might be, to gather clues about who they are. How do they eat, what do they eat? Do they think about food a lot? What do your characters' refrigerators look like? Not that any of this ever has to make it to the page, but it's a window into their character. I mean, when Rocky gets up at 4 a.m. and drinks four raw eggs,

---

*The following list is derived from Aristotle's other writings, mainly *De Anima* (*On the Soul*).

isn't that worth a gazillion pages of psychological notes on him? That image is so powerful and evocative that you know without further elaboration that he is serious about this boxing match. Look at Lester Burnham. What does he eat? By the end of his transformation from miserable mid-life-crisis guy to seeker of eternal youth, he's blending and drinking health drinks. What could tell us more about Lester's new attitude toward life? What could make Lester seem more human?

2. **Desiring Life.** At the heart of all action is the desire of the hero. Basic human desire is really what makes characters come alive on the screen. In *The Godfather*, when Michael Corleone goes to Italy and falls in love with an Italian woman from the mountains, doesn't that make him seem truly alive? It's a probable incident that flows with the action, reflecting his deep commitment to his Italian "roots." In *Gladiator,* Maximus yearns to go home to his family and, after they have been murdered, to join them in eternity. In *The Blair Witch Project*, the kids' ambition to tape the Blair Witch and make a film leads them to their death. Desiring is at the heart of what it means to be a living, breathing human being.

3. **Sensitive Life.** It goes without saying that our five senses are a big part of being alive. If a human being faces the prospect of losing sight or hearing, it's devastating. In fact, all of the five senses—sight, hearing,

touch, smell, and taste—define our lives at the most basic level. Lester Burnham spends a lot of time masturbating, doesn't he? In fact, it's how we are first introduced to him. What more do we need to sense that Lester is real and to "know" who he is? In cinema, perhaps the most important sense in regard to character development is visual perception. Great screenwriters know how to feed information to the audience through the eyes of characters, such as when Lester sees Angela at the pep rally and fantasizes about her. Showing how characters actually see things with their own eyes enables the audience to experience "causes" of the action. It also puts to use a powerful aspect of the cinematic medium, which is the hero's literal point of view.

4. **Locomotion.** Carefully depicting movement is vital to a screenplay. For example, *The Blair Witch Project* is a tapestry of rest and locomotion, in which the characters' use of their eyes and ears is also notably important. Heather, the lead character in the story, spends a lot of time running around, screaming, and trying to videotape the ground in front of her. The lifelike aspect of all the characters is transmitted largely by their physical movement, as they trudge through the woods.

5. **Capacity for Rational Thought.** Thinking about the mind and thought processes of people can be a fun way to brainstorm characters into existence. In *Annie Hall*,

Alvie is a rational man who has bouts of irrationality. This surfaces when a cop pulls him over and he tears up his license. In *Titanic* Rose jumps from the lifeboat to return to Jack, a slightly more irrational than rational act—but hey, this is a love story, and romantic love is rooted as much in animal nature as it is in the higher mind. (Rose is also slightly larger than life, and she's being consistent with what we've seen of her.)

In summary, to create a real human being for an audience you must have them do things that convince the audience that they are alive, *really* alive, giving details that even a scientist like Aristotle would appreciate.

27.

Dialog Is a Piece
of the Action

*. . . the poet must be more the poet of his stories
or Plots than of his verses, inasmuch as he is a poet
by virtue of the imitative element in his work, and
it is actions that he imitates.*

Like everything else in his system, dialog, which Aristotle calls "diction," should be part of the action. For Aristotle it's more important to strive to build a tight structure than it is to digress in the effort to compose beautiful dialog that isn't part of the main action:

> One will have much better success with a tragedy
> which, however inferior in these respects [dialog], has a
> Plot, a combination of incidents . . .

I've covered screenplays where the writers will start off with great dialog, but by the middle of the script I'm already bored. I later examine some of the mid-point dialog and it seems of the same quality as the beginning dialog. What's wrong? The same thing that's always wrong: The plot has not been adequately built. Dialog is part of the action and gets its power from the plot, whose effect builds in a *cumulative* as well as linear way. Dialog forms story action and derives life and energy from the action it helps build. This is a symbiotic relationship. For a simple demonstration, if I say the line, "They're here," it's not a great line of dialog. But in *Poltergeist*, when it's the young child announcing the arrival of a house full of ghosts, it's brilliant, because it's concise but moves us into a new stage of the plot (we now want to find out exactly *what*'s "here" and why this child is so attuned to the new invisible guests).

Aristotle goes so far as to say that although dialog is a building block of a drama, it can sometimes get in the way:

> Elaborate Diction, however, is required in places where there is no action, and no Character or Thought to be revealed. Where there is Character or Thought, on the other hand, an over-ornate Diction tends to obscure them.

Not only can elaborate dialog obscure thought, sometimes dialog that is "straight on the nose" can ruin a scene when characters say exactly what is on their minds and there is no sub-text to what they are saying. In *Gladiator*, in the scene where Maximus and Lucilla flirt in the garden, we sense an intense unstated sexual undercurrent to their words. But their dialog is not "on the nose," it's what's going on inside their minds that's intriguing to us. What's not said, or the inner thoughts of the characters, is often more dynamic to an audience, so it's not a good idea to have characters saying *exactly* what's on their minds but to use dialog to imply what they are thinking.

That's not to say that conversational dialog isn't important—audiences love dialog like that in *Pulp Fiction* or *Night on Earth*. I love dialog more than the average moviegoer, and my own scripts and films are dialog heavy. However, in even the most dialog-dependent script like *My Dinner with Andre*, the dialog is intrinsic to the action—to the plot, meaning, causality of the incidents, and dramatic unity. In fact, sometimes plot action *does* require that dialog be "on the nose," as in *Gladiator*, when Maximus gives his gladiator team clear instructions on how to fight the coming onslaught of enemy gladiators. Aristotle stresses the importance of language at every level of drama:

> The Thought of the persons in a play is shown in all that must be effected by their language—in every effort to prove or disprove, to arouse emotion (pity, fear, anger, and the like), or to exaggerate or minimize things.

However, language can be tricky. If actions speak louder than words, they can also speak better:

> The only difference is that in action the effect has to be produced without explanation; whereas with the spoken word it has to be produced by the speaker, and result from his language. What, indeed, would be the

good of the speaker, if things appeared in the required light even apart from anything he says?

Aristotle's system of thought includes a concept called "dialectic." Sounds like "dialog," doesn't it? That's because the two concepts are indeed similar. Let's see how they work.

First, someone makes a statement, a "thesis." Then an opposing statement is made, an "*anti*-thesis." These two statements then collide in opposition, forming a synthesis, which is kind of a "we start all over again" thesis:

JOE: (THESIS) We won't make it there because you're driving like my grandmother.
BOB: (ANTITHESIS) Your grandmother's dead.
JOE: (SYNTHESIS) Exactly!

Notice that in this exchange, Joe makes a statement that Bob is driving like his grandmother. Bob doesn't just respond, he uses the information contained in Joe's statement to make an opposing statement, that Bob's grandmother "is dead." This is an antithesis: Dead grandmothers can't drive. Joe then takes the mini-argument that's taken shape and "synthesizes" it into a new statement, "Exactly," which clarifies Joe's real message, that Bob's driving is fatally flawed. It's a fusion of the two ideas, that Bob drives like Joe's grandmother, and that Joe's grandmother is dead. Notice that what gets batted back and forth is simply information.

Here, dialog is a kind of fight that uses information in the last statement, and opposes it and moves the fight forward. Dialog as dialectic is, in effect, action. Compare the previous exchange to mere conversation:

JOE: We won't make it because you drive like my grand-mother.

BOB: I'm hungry.

JOE: I hope this car don't break down.

Obviously, this is more typical of two friends talking in that neither listens to the other. It's mere conversation, and does not move the action along.

Of course, you can blend dialetical and conversational dialog any way you want:

JOE: We won't make it there because you're driving like my grandmother.

BOB: Your grandmother's dead.

JOE: Exactly!

BOB: She is? I was just kidding.

BOB: Death is weird . . . isn't it?

JOE: Don't get deep on me. I think we should start looking for a motel.

BOB: Yeah. Do you know anything about computers?

JOE: Keep your eyes on the road.

BOB: I will. Do you wanna drive after lunch?

This exchange mixes dialectical dialog with a mere conversation to help create realistic dialog that moves the action of
the story along but allows a pause in it as well.

Dialog is sometimes dialectic, sometimes conversation.
But it is always action or part of the action. Do your best
to make your characters' language derive its power from the
cumulative whole of the living plot. You won't regret it.

28.

If the Pitch Doesn't Fill Me with Horror and Pity, the Movie Won't Either

The Plot in fact should be so framed that, even without seeing the things take place, he who simply hears the account of them shall be filled with horror and pity at the incidents . . .

Aristotle tells us that just by being told the basic plot, listeners should be moved by it, just as they would be when watching it enacted on the screen. What better way, then, to test whether your screenplay is going to do what you want it to do than to utter your ACTION-IDEA to people and see what kind of reaction it gets? Dramatic story is first and foremost an oratorical art; the incidents have to sound good to the ear (and mind) if they are going to entertain for any length of time.

Consider the independent-film success *The Blair Witch Project*, where you never see the witch. That's because the makers of that movie had the insight to understand the oratorical aspect of dramatic storytelling. The incidents of the movie *sounded* so gripping and scary that they spread over the Internet like wildfire and later by word of mouth at colleges. It all worked because the basic plot, or ACTION-IDEA, of *The Blair Witch Project* was so strong that people felt compelled to see the movie. In fact, they were scared *before* they saw the movie!

The Blair Witch Project had the luxury (as well as the genius) of using a mock documentary format whereby local residents are interviewed about the legend of the Blair Witch, who would make one kid face the wall while she killed the other and then kill the one facing the wall. Admit it, you felt something, even if you hate horror. That scenario gets played out at the end, when it happens to the two remaining kids: Michael faces the wall as Heather is killed. But the incident has already been implanted in our minds, which makes the replay of the incident at the end more powerful.

To take another example, how would a teenager try to convince his peers to see *Something About Mary*? They would retell the hilarious story incidents they saw. Or, consider how many people walking the American streets today can make other people laugh by retelling the incidents in *A Christmas Story*? Haven't you done that? I have. I remember once I told my screenwriter friend the plot of *Green Card* (a couple has to pretend to be married so one can get his green card, and they fall in love). He said, "Oh wow." He was feeling the power of the whole story, just from hearing its ACTION-IDEA.

Story has always been an oratorical art. Long ago, people sat around the fire, telling stories to each other for information and entertainment. The printing press, books, movies, and TV are relatively recent developments in the human scheme of things. But how we appreciate the essence of a story hasn't changed. We sound it out in our minds to enjoy it. It's that simple. That's why if it sounds good to people before we write it, it *is* good. Saying your idea out loud should produce whatever effect you want it to have on screen, or on the page. This is why the "pitch" is so important to everybody. Let's face it, the pitch is just the ACTION-IDEA sounded out loud. And if yours doesn't grab people the way *The Blair Witch Project*'s grabbed millions of fans, your screenplay won't either.

29.

The Non-Linear Soul of
Quentin Tarantino

*The Plot, in our present sense of the term, is
simply this, the combination of the incidents or
things done in the story . . .*

This chapter will look at the style of the highly original
screenwriter Quentin Tarantino. We'll examine a very
interesting aspect of his masterpiece, *Pulp Fiction*, which is
its "non-linear" plot. Playing with a story's time line might
be something you want to think about when starting to build
your screenplay's outline. This style of plot is very prevalent
in today's cinema.

While the *Poetics* doesn't directly address time-bending
plots per se, it's not a big stretch from Aristotle's "arrange-
ment of the incidents" to the plot rearranging that
characterizes many non-linear narratives. But it's important
to understand that non-linear plots are not composed of
simple flashbacks or told as memory or recollection. Their
chronological shuffling must work to create *meaning*, and
jolts in the movie's time line must call attention to themselves
(and better be used for a good reason!). Now let's examine
a brilliant chronological rearrangement of plot incidents.

In the first scene of *Pulp Fiction*, we find Honey Bunny and Pumpkin robbing a diner. The story moves on and different sub-actions with other characters occur, one showing Vince getting killed. Then the story returns to a time when Vince and Jules recover Marcellus's stolen money from drug dealers again. The action jumps right to Jules's speech, which he quotes from the Old Testament before killing the drug dealers. This is the first time in the "chronological story" that Jules launches into this speech but the second time in the story we see it. This speech is the pivot and handle of the whole non-linear structure.

In effect, *Pulp Fiction* takes the middle of the chronological story and slices it into the beginning and end of the plot, giving the movie a unique twist whereby banal conversation (the funny dialog in the rest of the story) is contrasted with Jules's urgent renunciation of his criminal life and his quoting of powerful passages from the Old Testament.

Perhaps the reason Tarantino is able to be convincing with his unique style of plot bending is because in all his writing he says what he really feels, from his own unique perspective. To understand what I mean, consider the following *Poetics* passage:

> As far as may be, too, the poet should even act his story with the very gestures of his personages. Given some natural qualifications, he who feels the emotions described will be the most convincing; distress and anger,

for instance, are portrayed most truthfully by one who is feeling them at the moment.

Quentin Tarantino is great at what he does because there is an "authentic feel" to his movies: They seem to come right from his heart and soul. Many people have tried to emulate his style, but the results have been weak. Not that Tarantino hasn't tapped into other films for his own ideas, but he manages to blend his own knowledge of other films and genres in a unique way.

You, too, have to find your soul and tap into it. It might not be quite as marketable as Tarantino's, but at the end of the day, Aristotle would rather see you writing something powerful from your own soul than trying to reproduce someone else's cool style. As a story analyst, so would I.

Don't try to second-guess what the Hollywood market is looking for. I'll tell you a little secret that is not such a secret. In Hollywood, they don't know what they are looking for. They know it when they see it. This is not to knock Hollywood, because, as William Goldman said, "Nobody knows anything. Nobody knows a goddam thing." It's also not to say go ahead and write something completely idiosyncratic, and wonder why a studio doesn't want to invest 100 million dollars to produce your fantasy. Instead you should attempt to write from your soul and move an audience in a way that comes naturally, but you must have "moving your audience" as your ultimate end; everything else should fall into place. Gene Wilder has been quoted as saying that his overall guideline for knowing what to write is simply this: "I am going to the movies tonight. Would I want to see this?"

Regardless of whether you write drama, comedy, horror, science fiction, or action, find out what you write best, and guess what—your range is probably limited. I've talked to professional screenwriters who have said that the kinds of scripts they write aren't what they'd wanted to write. It's hard to write a good script, not to mention sell it, which Aristotle, unfortunately, says nothing about. But if you can zero in on one kind of genre, you stand a better chance of developing it to the highest level possible and breaking through with it. Be aware of what you are actually trying to accomplish with your scripts. What kind of scripts are you trying to write, and why do you think they fit in? There are certain kinds of scripts that come more naturally to me than others. It has to do with who I am and what I like. Just be honest with yourself, experiment, and be aware. It will probably save you lots of time.

Instead of "write what you know," Aristotle is telling you to write what you can truly feel, or truly experience in your heart. Have readings with actors or friends who can read your screenplays back to you, attentively and spirit-edly—it will give you a feel for your work. It's probably no coincidence that Quentin Tarantino also is an actor.

Again, whether you use a non-linear plot or not, write to express your unique self. And always try to communicate to an audience and move them *as* an audience. Write from your soul for an audience, not for your favorite esoteric film director in Sweden.

30.

If Your Story Were a Musical, Where Would the Numbers Be?

From the point of view, however, of its quantity, i.e. the separate sections into which it is divided, a tragedy has the following parts: Prologue, Episode, Exode, and a choral portion . . .

In Aristotle's day, tragedy had music at its core, the chorus sang and danced. Tragedy grew out of music:

It [tragedy] certainly began in improvisations—as did also Comedy; the one originating with the prelude to the Dithyramb, the other with the prelude to the phallic songs, which still survive as institutions in many of our cities.

The dramatic arts grew out of an early religious ritualistic chanting called "dithyramb," a primitive musical art. In some ways, as a result, Greek tragedy resembles an extended song or symphony, as the following passage from the *Poetics* points out:

The Prologue is all that precedes the Parode of the chorus; an Episode is all that comes in between two whole choral songs; the Exode all that follows after the last choral song. In the choral portion the Parode is the whole of the first utterance of the chorus; a Stasimon, a song of the chorus without anapests or trochees [dances]; a *Commos*, a lamentation sung by chorus and actor in concert.

Here Aristotle gives clues about how a screenwriter might use song and the structure of music in shaping a screenplay. For example, the "prologue" in Greek drama ties back story (what happens before the opening scene) to the front story (story after the movie begins) and gives space before the "first cause" of action can be born. "Episodes" are blocks of scenes; "choral songs" are statements of the chorus that occur at regular intervals; and "Commos" is an ancient Greek theatrical term for scenes that involve inter-actions between the actor and the chorus.

The "parode" was the first song of the chorus, and—note the similarity of the two words—a kind of "parody" of the action to come, a preview or transition during which the chorus came out and made their whole "first statement of action" and warmed up the audience. A simple example of a parode is the scene in *The Godfather* where the Hollywood producer finds a severed horse's head in his bed, a warning from the Don about what might happen to him if Johnny Fontaine doesn't get a part in his next movie. This scene is not quite a prologue, and the main action (Sollozzo having the Don shot) hasn't begun yet. It's in effect a "parody" of action; it foreshadows how action works in the world of *The Godfather*.

For a brief example of "parodies" of action, recall the scene in *The Terminator* where the title character rips out the heart of the teenage hoodlum. It's not quite prologue anymore (the prologue tells the future), and it's not the "first cause" of action, which is the Terminator killing the first Sarah Conner. However, this scene helps the prologue smoothly dissolve into the beginning of the main action, making the rhythm and movement of action easier to digest for the audience. They get to see "how" action works, before they experience the what and why of the story's action.

Remember, a "parode," as it's used here, is a convention of Greek tragedy that has evolved into some modern movies as a tendency more than an overarching story principle. Think of it as an extra tool, but be careful! Don't throw off your story's tone by trying to toss in a "Weird Al Yankovic" mockery of your action; that's not what parode is all about.

Even now, dramatic story functions like a song or symphony with "refrains" or repetition. The action builds in a cumulative as well as a linear manner. Not only does plot information pile up piece by piece, but the scenes add to our understanding of the movie's particular world, thus making it easier for the audience to connect with the characters. It's all done to build the intensity of the work without adding plot lines that complicate what the audience must retain and focus on.

Greek tragedy had an easy time doing this because of the convention of the chorus. During *Oedipus Rex,* the chorus would come out in intervals and sing and chant different long, beautiful, haunting passages (pleasurable accessories) without advancing the plot one iota. However, the chorus developed the magnitude of the story, making it seem more frightening, more intense, and more real. It evoked a strong sense of the gods. Think of it this way: If one or two actors stand around the stage and say, "Oedipus, the gods are after you. You're in trouble," that's only a little scary. On the other hand, if a line of 100 chorus members sing and chant, questioning the "meaning" of Apollo's prediction about Oedipus's fate over and over again *without* advancing the plot, isn't this scarier? Isn't this design more effective than having the plot throw on more and more linear incidents that must be absorbed by the audience? The simple ACTION-IDEA of *Oedipus Rex* is "present," or "sensed" in every syllable of the chorus's "statements," without these statements adding to the plot.

We see here, as we saw earlier, that the ends (plot) are always in the means (scenes), with a new perspective added. We see how plot is a living creature and how scenes are "organs" that develop its magnitude and depth. How does this relate to the musical structure of ancient tragedy?

While we generally no longer use a chorus per se (there are exceptions, e.g., *Something About Mary*) we use alternatives to it. A "chorus" doesn't have to be actual people commenting on the action. Images can make comments as well. In the masterpiece *Angel Heart,* the "chorus," or what serves the role of the chorus, is achieved by using a series of repetitious flashbacks from the point of view of the hero (Harry Angel) as he remembers his past incarnation as Johnny Favorite. The audience sees these flashbacks as well, which recall the horrible deeds he did in order to steal Harry's soul and identity. These images comment on Harry's past behavior and raise a number of questions: "What is Harry remembering? What do these memories that keep occurring have to do with this horrible evil he is starting to uncover in the present? What kind of person is Harry, and how will he pay for his past deeds?"

Angel Heart uses repetitious *images* to comment on the action, a perfect example of the ways in which a film can expand on the basic dramatic storytelling tools from Aristotle's day. In cinema, visuals and/or sound effects can help to develop the magnitude of the simple plot in the same way that a chorus raised issues for the audience to ponder during an ancient theatrical tragedy performance.

Dramatic story is indeed like song. All intense dramatic stories build toward the hero's change in fortune both in a linear and songlike cumulative fashion with "refrains" as variations and repetitions of the ACTION-IDEA. Perhaps a better analogy is to say that a dramatic story resembles a song or symphony but still imitates life. We have much to learn from musical composition in terms of dramatic storytelling, but what little I've revealed to you here can work nothing short of miracles for the average screenplay.

31.

History Repeats Itself . . .
Real and Imagined

. . . what convinces is the possible; now whereas
we are not yet sure as to the possibility of that
which has not happened, that which has happened
is manifestly possible, else it would not have come to
pass.

As a script reader, I'm surprised screenwriters don't use history more often to give a "framework" to their stories, as well as a flavor of reality. This tool really works, because as Aristotle was well aware, using the past helps convince the audience of the reality of your story, because elements of it have really happened. Don't kid yourself—making your audience believe in the reality of your story is an important aspect of screenwriting.

In Aristotle's system, the use of history takes different forms, depending on the form and purpose of your screenplay. Past historic events, or even recent current events, can serve to buttress its realism. Christopher Columbus discovering America is history. The Presidential voting crisis in 2000 is history. All that matters in terms of "using" history as a framework is that the events happened. Now, for a neat little trick that professional screenwriters know, consider this: A gold mine awaits you in the dusty untapped archives of the library, if you dig deep enough. Here, forgotten stories lie that may never have made the headlines but because they are based on reality, they have a flavor to them . . . a bite. A good example of this is *Boogie Nights*, a modern masterpiece based loosely on the life of a real porn star who was very much like the lead character, Dirk Diggler, from the man's special physical "endowment" to the violent drug-related escapades he gets involved with as the story develops. Even the most obscure story will have a certain vibe to it if it really happened. It will just feel real. It convinces because it is possible, and is possible because it happened.

Another good way to use history is to incorporate into your screenplay that which has become absorbed into society as common myth and legend. For example, there is the famous legend that the mafia got Frank Sinatra the role in *From Here to Eternity*—whether or not this is true is irrelevant. *The Godfather* alludes to this piece of "history," when Don Corleone "entices" the movie producer to give Johnny Fontaine a role. Whether or not the audience is aware of this myth when watching *The Godfather* is also irrelevant. What matters is that the scenes feel real.

Much of *Gladiator* is based on ancient history. There was a Caesar named Commodus, who had irksome dealings with a gladiator Maximus. There were gladiator stars, underground cells where they lived and trained, and many were slaves. Researching historical periods can give a writer inspiration and his screen play narrative cogency. Another way to use history in your screenplay is to write about true events, as James Cameron did with his mega-hit, *Titanic*. Then there is of course *Citizen Kane*, which is a very direct/ indirect reference to newspaper tycoon William Randolph Hearst. These are obvious applications of history as a framework to convince your audience of your story.

Quentin Tarantino is a genius for triggering a sense of "history" in his films by referring to old movies. *Swingers* constantly refers to *The Godfather* and *Goodfellas*. In a sense, they are history to us because we've all seen them, and hence these movies are a part of our shared reality.

Whether you revive a forgotten hero from the Civil War or have your characters reference and recite lines from a Farrelly Brothers' movie, history is a powerful tool that can be used in many ways to enrich your screenplay. Somehow, history works like magic, and as screenwriters we need all the magic we can get!

32

Aristotle's Take on the Importance of Drama

It is clear that the general origin of poetry was due to two causes, each of them part of human nature. Imitation is natural to man from childhood, one of his advantages over the lower animals being this, that he is the most imitative creature in the world, and learns at first by imitation. And it is also natural for all to delight in works of imitation. The truth of this second point is shown by experience: though the objects themselves may be painful to see, we delight to view the most realistic representations of them in art, the forms for example of the lowest animals and of dead bodies. The explanation is to be found in a further fact: to be learning something is the greatest pleasure not only to the philosopher but also to the rest of mankind, however small their capacity for it; the reason of the delight in seeing pictures is that one is at the same time learning—gathering the meaning of things, e.g. that the man there is so-and-so . . .

In this excerpt, Aristotle explains why dramatic works are such an important part of our culture. Imitation is a crucial learning tool for human beings, and it is also something that we continue to enjoy in adulthood through reading or watching drama. It's part of our human nature to both learn from and enjoy imitative works of art, but Aristotle further suggests that suffering can be an important element to add to a dramatic story. Not only does this appeal to the less savory side of human nature, but it also helps us face what both terrifies and fascinates us: death.

Throughout the *Poetics*, Aristotle suggests that in his day, watching a hero suffer is what the audience paid for when it went to the theater. Granted, modern dramatics have evolved so that they can hold audiences' attention through more subtle and less macabre plot lines, but this principle still holds true. Vicariously experiencing the hero's suffering, as well as the final cathartic release, is a major part of how drama works. (There are fluffy movies that combine elements of drama and comedy, but as we'll see later, comedy is created with an *absence* of suffering.)

In today's cinema, a story can compensate for lack of physical suffering and/or death by including intense emotional or psychological suffering, the way Ingmar Bergman's *Through a Glass Darkly* and Elia Kazan's *A Streetcar Named Desire* do. Both display mental anguish and are as riveting as any Greek tragedy because in each, the hero's suffering is of such magnitude that it's as painful as when Oedipus gouges his eyes out—and as gripping for an audience.

In much of Aristotle's philosophy, he alludes to the belief that we are simultaneously animals and higher spiritual beings. Our desire to develop our intelligent and rational side is counterbalanced with our animalistic pleasure in watching suffering and death. The key to great screenplays (think *Gladiator*) is finding a way to combine both elements so each side of our human nature is satisfied. So as you sit down and stare at your blank screen, pretend to your heart's content. But add a little suffering, pain, or death so your audience pretends along with you, unless this truth has turned you off to movies and screenwriting completely. Then we'll suffer and learn without your help!

33.

Aristotle Took Comedy Seriously

> *. . . Comedy, it is (as has been observed) an imitation of men worse than the average; worse, however, not as regards any and every sort of fault, but only as regards one particular kind, the Ridiculous, which is a species of the Ugly. The Ridiculous may be defined as a blunder or deformity not productive of pain or harm to others; the mask, for instance, that excites laughter, is something ugly and distorted without causing pain.*

There once existed a whole section in the *Poetics* that broke down how comedy works, which unfortunately is lost forever. But in the version of the *Poetics* that has survived, Aristotle does say *some* things about comedy, *and* talks about it at length, which can mean one thing: He took it seriously! The fact that he treated it seriously means that like tragedy and epic, comedy is a significant genre and worthy of some analysis.

First things first. Comedy is to make the audiences laugh, which means we must minimize suffering. Aristotle speaks of comedy as the "comic mask," "ugly and distorted," but not painful, in fact, when there is pain and death and suffering in comedy, we call it "black comedy." But without suffering, it's desirable to have the characters be somehow distorted (either physically or emotionally) so we can laugh at them. Think for example of some of the rubber-face characters that Jim Carrey has played in, say, *Ace Ventura*, or classics like the Marx Brothers comedies, etc. That's Aristotle's notion of comedy. Something like *Galaxy Quest* is more sophisticated, actually more like a "drama" with jokes and a happy ending.

For a specimen Aristotelian comedy, I'd like to use *Road Trip* because it's what I imagine as the perfect *Poetics* comedy. First of all, Aristotle tells us in the excerpt that there must be "bad" persons. He doesn't mean "evil" persons, but lowlifes—goofy or laughable people. Aristotle knew that if morality got too heavy in a comic story, the audiences might not laugh. *Road Trip* is able to achieve laughable characters who are not lowlifes as much as they are laughable in their attitudes and disposition about life, especially sex (they are just college kids). Of course, there is Barry Manilow (Tom Green), who is the perpetual student, completely odd, and clearly "below the line" of having any virtue the audience will relate to. Yet the character is funny. Barry Manilow narrates the story to the future college applicants who come to listen to him talk about why they should choose his school for their college career. Instead of talking about a great academic department or sports teams, he decides to reveal the escapades of four students who took a road trip. The trip was done on the fly to retrieve a videotape his friend Josh made of having sex with a girl, which was mailed to his steady girlfriend by mistake. That's the plot of *Road Trip*, its ACTION-IDEA. While there is one main plot, there is also a "double issue," as Aristotle calls it. As the boys go on the road, Barry stays home to feed Mitch, a pet snake of Kyle's, one of the guys who departs on the road trip. Barry tells his story to the "chorus" and interjects his own unrelated story of his failed attempts to feed the snake a tiny white mouse. The scenes of Barry trying to feed the snake are hilarious and *do* fracture the unity, but it works because according to Aristotle, a comedic plot doesn't have to be as tight:

> After this comes the construction of Plot which some rank first, one with a double story (like the *Odyssey*) and an opposite issue for the good and the bad personages. It is ranked as first only through the weakness of the audiences; the poets merely follow their public, writing as its wishes dictate. But the pleasure here is not that of Tragedy. It belongs rather to Comedy.

So it's not just acceptable in comedy to have double plotting, sub-plotting, even episodic plotting, it's a necessary part of comedic structure. It's better to keep comedy loose. Aristotle sees comedy as more of a crowd-pleasing art.

Comedy still requires a unified action and heroes with goals. Even the snake-feeding episodes converge with the main plot, as Beth catches Barry trying to feed the snake and learns how to get in touch with Josh in order to warn him about his final exam.

In *Road Trip*, there is a strong main plot that carries most of the action, but there is this double issue as well. Comedy uses the tools of the dramatic structure but it shapes a looser and more episodic plot so the jokes can carry it. The tight tragic structure in some ways adds too much tension for humor. That doesn't mean comedy isn't plotted; it just means that a tight structure or ONE COMPLETE ACTION isn't as important. There can be episodic linkage of scenes, double issues, etc.

To take another look at *Road Trip*, there is a "first cause" of action, which is Josh having sex with Beth even though he has a steady girlfriend. There is cause-and-effect action because once the tape is mailed out accidentally, it causes them to go on the road trip. There are incidents of necessity, where they go to a sperm bank to donate sperm to get money to continue traveling, etc. Much of what happens on the road is haphazard and links each scene chronologically. However, the sequence of events is presented as a probable chain of events. And the action does form a continuous whole, ONE COMPLETE UNIFIED ACTION, but a little looser than a tragic structure needs to be. The point is that in comedy, plot is not soul. Character is soul. There is even room for discoveries and reversals of fortune in comedy, but don't make the plot too tight, or too morally heavy.

If you dig comedy, go for it. You can create brilliant dramatic comedies that are structured like tragedies but have lots of jokes, like *Bottle Rocket* (downbeat ending, though).

In writing comedies, use the same tools you would use in writing drama, but keep the structure loose because it aids the humor. Eliminate real suffering unless it's black comedy. Comedy's goal is *not* to make the audience weep and understand truth in the tragic way. It's to make them laugh, and understand truth in the comedic way. If done correctly, this can be deeper and more powerful than any dramatic story.

Use the Principles from the *Poetics* to Play with and Against the Audience's Expectations

The hardest aspect of writing this book was that every time I wrote about a screenwriting principle from the *Poetics*, a movie would immediately pop into my head that defied it. For example, in one of my favorite independent movies of all time, *Slacker*, there is absolutely no causal relationship between any of the scenes. But then I would realize, that's just the point: The film's flouting of viewers' expectations is done on purpose, and it works like gang-busters. Aristotle's principle of causal connection still functions, implied by its very absence! Jim Jarmusch's work *Stranger Than Paradise* is very episodic at times, but you sense he's *aware* that he is being that way, and he's playing against the audience's belief that a plot should be causally related. David Lynch's work is brilliant, but sometimes I cannot ascertain what the "causes" of the action are, or what is going on at all, yet it still works. I could go on and on cataloging how some great movies seem to work against the principles of dramatic structure, but you get the point. You've got to know the rules in order to break them. You're trying to work with and against the audience's expectations. There is nothing more delightful on earth than reading a screenplay that breaks the "rules" and works. That's the point of studying the principles, to give you flexibility.

To me, the amazing thing about the *Poetics* is that for all the aspects of good screenwriting the *Poetics* addresses, it does not address everything directly. For example, take conflict. Everybody knows conflict is important, and it's probably the dominant mode of action. Greek tragedy was loaded with conflict, so it's safe to say Aristotle assumed (as we can about movie storytelling) that conflict is a given. He was more concerned with what's not so easy to understand, which is unifying action, making the "causes" of the action clear, making a real moral character revealed in a way that makes the audience relate to them.

The *Poetics* can't tell you everything about writing an immortal screenplay, but it's a great place to start. Take the principles that Aristotle laid out and use them to analyze movies you like and try and figure out why they work. Even if you don't agree with a single tenet from the *Poetics*, you must come up with your own analysis of cinematic story to construct your own method. I don't believe in the myth of the genius who rolls out of bed and creates a masterpiece without breaking a sweat. I'm a Thomas Edison "genius is 99 percent perspiration" believer. All artists, including great screenwriters, have adopted some personalized form of studying film and have cataloged in their brains techniques that work. That's what I have tried to do here using the

Poetics, following what Aristotle tried to do with the dramatic art of his day.

So, please, by all means, try putting these concepts, which I fondly think of as Movie Poetics, to use. Don't just say, "Yeah, you bet, an ACTION-IDEA." Write one. Try to come up with a three-sentence mini-story that works the way Aristotle taught us. Think about using a tragic deed to create a center of gravity in your story. Connect all your action through probable and necessary cause-and-effect action in a way that builds a story that feels like reality and could be possible. Find a unique way to build to a reversal of fortune and discovery moment, including connecting it to a tragic deed in the back story. Find a spicy moral contradiction at the heart of your conflict that will color your hero's actions, and connect your audiences' psyches to the center of the hero's soul. To create your screenplay's moral universe, find the perfect intermediate character between good and evil in a way that will make the balance between those forces riveting. Have your hero represent the ground zero of goodness, and then orchestrate characters above and below the line.

Remember, poet means "maker." You, the screenwriter-poet, make something, just like a builder makes a house. As a screenwriter, you are a builder of plots. What that means is that I'd rather see you spend months figuring out a powerful structure for your story than creating great dialog that doesn't build a great plot. It's like painting beautiful shingles with no house to hang them onto.

If I can add another two cents to all this (which is inspired by none other than Aristotle's other writings), let me say this: Be sensible about your writing life and general health. I know aspiring screenwriters who get drunk because Ernest Hemingway did. They think drinking, drugs, and abusing their bodies is a part of the writing life. It's not. Writing requires unbelievable physical energy, massive commitment from your body, heart-soul-mind, and emotions. Most of us have to work day jobs while we're trying to write that screenplay, so it's doubly important that you keep your temple sacred as you attack the writing beast.

Lastly, write from your soul. Your real soul. As a story analyst, I have rarely seen really "bad" scripts come through the pipeline. I would simply call them really mediocre. I'm starting to believe that the proliferation of mediocrity has to do more with the fact that many writers are trying to second-guess the Hollywood system, which is a very tough system to write for indeed. That's why I tell writers, especially those trying to break in, write from your soul. That way, the powers that be may sense something they like in your script, something they want to use. The trick to writing from your soul is the essence of the *Poetics*. You must communicate your soul to an audience *and* move that audience, as a whole. Whatever journey you want to take your audience on, you must decide at some point where you want to take them, how to take them there, and *then* take them there. But always remember, as a screenwriter, you are a builder of plots, complete actions that can move a viewer to new heights of emotions, and hence give clarity and insight into *being human*, which is the sum total of all the actions a person must take to register as a part of the universe. I think what Aristotle's *Poetics* essentially teaches us is how to depict the human condition through action, which is a powerful way to "say" truth—without spouting rhetoric the way I am now.

Bare your soul in a simple, easy-to-understand way that, because of its sheer honesty, will be more unique than any flavor of the moment you have chosen to write your screenplay about. Bend the "rules" to your heart's content. Don't worry . . . they won't break. First just learn what they are—in your mind, in your heart, and in your soul.